A MATTER OF MINUTES
THE ENDURING LEGACY OF BLOODY SUNDAY

JOANNE O'BRIEN is an Irish photojournalist who lives and works in London. Her work has been published in Britain and Ireland as well as internationally. She is a founder member of the London-based agency, FORMAT Photographers.

Born in Dublin of Catholic and Protestant parents, she studied history at University College Dublin before taking up photography. She worked as co-author on *Across the Water* (Virago Press, 1988) which was the first book-length study of Irish women's emigration to Britain.

She specialises in portraiture and social documentary and her work encompasses a wide range of social and cultural issues. Her work was selected for inclusion in the recent *Faces of the Century* show at the National Portrait Gallery, London.

A Matter of Minutes

The Enduring Legacy of Bloody Sunday

Joanne O'Brien

WOLFHOUND PRESS

Published in 2002 by
Wolfhound Press
An imprint of Merlin Publishing
16 Upper Pembroke Street, Dublin 2, Ireland
Tel: +353 1 676 4373; Fax: +353 1 676 4368
e-mail: publishing@merlin.ie
www.merlin-publishing.com

British Library Cataloguing in Publication Data
A catalogue record for this book is available from the British Library.

Quote on page 11 from James Baldwin *The Fire Next Time*, London:
Penguin, 1964, p.71

ISBN 1-903582-15-6

5 4 3 2 1

Cover photographs: Joanne O'Brien
Duotone separations: Colour Repro Ltd
Cover and book design: David Houlden
Typesetting: David Houlden
Printing: Zure S.A., Spain

To my parents, Denis and Iris, for the values they imparted

CONTENTS

ACKNOWLEDGEMENTS

A book like this could not happen without the support of many people. I particularly want to express my gratitude to all the people who gave interviews. Their bravery and willingness to evoke often harrowing memories made this book possible.

Special thanks must go to John Kelly and Michael McKinney and the Bloody Sunday Justice Campaign. They put me in touch with many of those whom I interviewed and were always available to answer my queries and to offer insights.

I would like to give special thanks to Mary Nelis who believed in the project from the beginning and whose heart and home have always been open. Her insights and suggestions were invaluable, as were those of her husband, Billy Nelis. My thanks to Betty and Michael Walker for all their help. Betty kindly invited me to meet the Bloody Sunday relatives socially at an early and crucial time.

I am grateful to Aileen O'Toole and Damien Kiberd of the *Sunday Business Post* who first published some of the interviews and to Heather Warnicker who did the design for the newspaper pieces.

My thanks must also go to Joe Parks for the funeral ticket he so generously entrusted to me for publication.

I am very grateful to Russell Jones for his work on the transcripts and comments on the edits and for his kindness and encouragement throughout.

I am also very grateful to Cheryl Aaron who read some of the early edits and made very useful comments.

My thanks to Sally Shovelin for setting me on the road to Derry.

Sincere thanks also to Corinne Turner for her suggestions and advice with the photographs.

And to Alan Pritchard for his generosity and all the wonderful discussions during the course of the work.

I would like to express particular thanks to Tony Murray for his work on the map and his huge support in reading the book and offering suggestions.

Other people to whom must go my sincerest thanks include:

Mary-Jane Anderton, Colm Barton, Denis Bradley, Liam Bradley, Lis Birrane, Jim Boumelha, Maurice Coakley, Patricia Coyle, Geraldine Doherty, John Donaghy, George Downey, Gerry Duddy, Geraldine Emsley, Martin Finucane, Fleet Photos, my colleagues at FORMAT Photographers, Geoffrey Frosh, Charles Grieve, Angela Hegarty, Eamonn Houston, Malcom Imrie, Fr John Irwin, Jarlath Kearney, David Kelly, Jo Klein, Paul Mahon, Helen Mahony, Patricia McBride, Cathleen and Manus McDaid, Deirdre McDaid, Dr Donal McDermott, Karen McElhinney, Michael McGuinness, Michael McKay, Fr George McLaughlin, Nòel McLoone, Don Mullan, John Nash, Cathy Nelis, Declan Nelis, Paddy Nelis, Áine Ní Orain, Ciaran Shields, Paddy and Anna Walsh.

Lastly, I would like to express my gratitude to David Houlden, my editor at Wolfhound, for his wonderful knowledge and the skill and passion he brought to the book.

D E R R Y

30 January 1972

B L O O D Y   S U N D A Y

DEAD	**INJURED**
PATRICK DOHERTY	MICHAEL BRADLEY
GERARD DONAGHEY	MICHAEL BRIDGE
JACKIE DUDDY	ALANA BURKE
HUGH GILMOUR	PATRICK CAMPBELL (NOW DECEASED)
JOHN JOHNSTON	MARGARET DEERY (NOW DECEASED)
MICHAEL KELLY	DAMIEN DONAGHEY
MICHAEL MCDAID	JOSEPH FRIEL
KEVIN MCELHINNEY	DANIEL GILLESPIE
BERNARD MCGUIGAN	JOSEPH MAHON
GERALD MCKINNEY	PATRICK MCDAID
WILLIAM MCKINNEY	DANIEL MCGOWAN
WILLIAM NASH	ALEXANDER NASH (NOW DECEASED)
JAMES WRAY	PATRICK O'DONNELL
JOHN YOUNG	MICHAEL QUINN

John Johnston, listed above as one of the Bloody Sunday dead, actually died on 16 June 1972,
as a result of the injuries he had sustained on 30 January.

To accept one's past — one's history — is not the same thing as drowning in it; it is learning how to use it. An invented past can never be used; it cracks and crumbles under the pressures of life like clay in a season of drought.

James Baldwin, *The Fire Next Time*, 1963

NOTICE IN DERRY TAXI, 1997

INTRODUCTION

When 15-year-old Damien 'Bubbles' Donaghey was shot in the right thigh one Sunday afternoon in 1972, he didn't know that he was the first of twenty-eight unarmed civilians to be killed or injured in Derry that January day.

Bloody Sunday happened thirty years ago and its significance has yet to be fully comprehended, even though its legacy has affected so many. It was a day on which numerous people in Derry had their Sunday dinner and took themselves off to a civil rights demonstration — Alana Burke, who was run over by a Saracen armoured car as she ran for safety, remembers 30 January 1972 as ' …bitterly cold, but a lovely and bright sunny day.' An estimated 15,000–20,000 people assembled — the largest march in the town up to that time — to protest against internment. This had been introduced a few months earlier, in August 1971, with the implementation of new legislation. In effect, it meant that citizens of Northern Ireland could be subjected to indefinite periods of imprisonment without charge or due process. On the day of its introduction, 342 Catholic men had been interned.[1]

Stories of brutality connected with the new legislation abounded, uniting non-unionist opinion of various shades in condemnation of the arbitrary arrests and the violence that was meted out to those in detention. It was the latest in a long line of increasingly repressive measures which had alienated and politicised the Catholic community of Northern Ireland. The brutal policing methods favoured by the unionist authorities and the issue of how public order itself was maintained had themselves become subjects of protest. These particular issues had risen to prominence after a civil rights demonstration about housing in Derry was attacked by the RUC in October 1968; a large-scale riot ensued.[2]

In August 1969, the community in the Bogside and Creggan set up 'Free Derry' after three days of fighting had broken out between residents and the police and loyalists. This short period of conflict became known as the Battle of the Bogside and, not for the first time, galvanised the community into a united defence. Barricades were built on all the thoroughfares into 'Free Derry' and it became a 'no-go' area for the police and the army. As a local GP, Dr Raymond McClean, put it, 'An entire community had been at war with what was supposed to have been their own police force … a community used to economic depression, emigration and hopelessness [was] now on its feet with a spring in its step.'[3]

But by August 1971, there was a general consensus in the Stormont and Westminster governments that Free Derry's secession from Northern Ireland was intolerable. Major General Ford, who took control of British Land

Forces in Northern Ireland in August 1971, made it very clear both privately and publicly that the Army would be taking tough measures. In January 1972, he was writing to his boss, Lieutenant-General Harry Tuzo, proposing that a number of what he termed 'Derry's Young Hooligans' (DYH) should be shot as a deterrent to other rioters. He discussed the use of lower-than-usual-calibre bullets, '... to enable ringleaders to be engaged with less lethal ammunition', and suggested that, 'The minimum force necessary to achieve a restoration of law and order is to shoot selected ringleaders among the DYH after clear warnings have been given.' A decision was taken to send the British Army's crack soldiers, the 1st Battalion Parachute Regiment, to Derry; their deployment was viewed with considerable apprehension. Lord Widgery later described this regiment in his report as the 'roughest and the toughest unit in Northern Ireland'.[4] It appears that the Paras ordered into the Bogside on Bloody Sunday were briefed that they were up against a formidable enemy, and told to act accordingly.

On Bloody Sunday the civil rights marchers congregated in Bishop's Field in Creggan on a hill overlooking the city. The demonstration had been called by the Northern Ireland Civil Rights Association (NICRA), who urged that the protest be peaceful. In addition, local IRA units had given an undertaking that all guns would be removed from the nationalist Bogside area through which the march would pass. Despite these actions, some people did have misgivings; many were concerned about what had occurred the week before at another civil rights protest on Magilligan Strand, outside the recently opened internment camp there. On that occasion, members of the Parachute Regiment had been very heavy-handed; their officers were forced to restore order by beating their own men back when they assaulted the demonstrators.

Many of those who had participated in the march on Bloody Sunday later described the jaunty air with which the parade set off that day, the winter sunshine taking the edge off the cold. In torrential rain, the atmosphere at the funerals which were held three days later was in total contrast to the optimism with which the march had begun. By the end of the afternoon of 30 January 1972, thirteen unarmed men lay dead; another was to die of his injuries within months, and fourteen others, including two women, were seriously wounded.

The aim of the marchers had been to make their protest peacefully in the city centre, at the Guildhall Square. In the event, they were barred by the Army from doing so and a group of perhaps 200 young men broke away from the march to throw stones at the Paratroopers at the Army barricade in William Street. As many observers and some participants later commented: it was 'nothing unusual for Derry at that time' — rioting occurred at that spot frequently. NICRA stewards were beginning to get the crowd to disperse when the army fired rubber bullets and CS gas. This was then followed up with water cannon which cleared the street; a minor riot was over.

In the meantime, as the afternoon was drawing to a close, the main body of the march reached its final destination in Rossville Street. Despite the cold, some 5,000 people were still in the area for the post-march rally at Free Derry Corner. It was addressed by civil-rights campaigners,

MPs and out-of-town dignitaries who stood on a flat-bed coal lorry. The time was approximately 4.10 p.m.

At this stage, people in the crowd were unaware that, about 20 minutes earlier, in William Street, Parachute Regiment snipers had shot teenager Damien Donaghey, and then Johnny Johnston, a 59-year-old businessman. The older man, who happened to be passing, was hit as he bent down to help the injured youngster.

The rally continued. Veteran pacifist Fenner Brockway was standing on the platform waiting to address the crowd when, without any warning, several armoured personnel carriers came speeding up the street and screeched to a halt. Witnesses later described how soldiers poured out of them and began firing live rounds. Total panic ensued as people dived for cover or ran for their lives. Many did not even hear the opening shots — or thought the sound was of rubber bullets being fired — but ran with the rest of the terrified crowd. Some saw others fall but, as Joe Friel put it later, 'It didn't compute' [that they were shot]. Others made tragic tactical errors and ran for shelter into the courtyards of the nearby flats where Paratroopers were already starting to take up position. People crowded through any open door they could reach, and nearby houses were soon packed. Some must have pushed past others in a frantic attempt to escape the shooting, and today live with the guilt of what visceral fear made them do. Kay Duddy, whose brother Jackie was the first to die that day, recently commented: 'Survivor guilt; it's a big thing in this town.'

The Army operation lasted approximately 27 minutes and commenced with General Ford standing at the barricade as his men poured through, waving his swagger stick and shouting: 'Go on the Paras!'[5] Like General Dyer, the British officer in command at Amritsar in 1919, Ford gave no warning to the crowd that his men were going to open fire.

After 25 minutes, the order to withdraw from the area was given. Following Bloody Sunday there was an escalation in violent conflict throughout Northern Ireland. John Kelly, who lost his brother Michael that day, commented: 'Approximately twenty minutes' work, cost the lives of hundreds of people.' Jim Wray, who was photographed staging his own one-man sit-down protest during the riot in William Street, died later that day. His brother Liam talks of the IRA recruitment that went on after Bloody Sunday, so great was the anger and outrage in the community.

The city of Derry was left in deep shock after the killings. Frances Gillespie, whose husband Daniel had a lucky escape, recalls, 'We didn't get to bed 'til all hours. You were trying to find out the names. I heard there was a young fellow Kelly [shot], and I knew his mammy and his sister. And then you heard about the others like young Duddy out of Rosemount.... There was a wild lot of people in the streets ... talking.' Businesses and schools were closed for three days and thousands attended the thirteen wakes that took place. As one woman put it, 'Derry was a wakehouse'. Another described how the carpet was worn through with people coming to the house.

At both community and personal levels, there followed the chaos so often associated with disasters which usually makes it even more difficult for victims to recover from such an event. The local hospital, Altnagelvin, was inundated with injured and dead. The morgue was overflowing — bodies had to be placed on the floor — and the operating theatres were full as medical staff tried to deal with the crisis.

The priests at the Cathedral parish house had people coming to their door all night, enquiring about missing relatives. The Army had arrested perhaps a hundred people and refused to release their names.

The funerals were arranged for the following Wednesday, except for that of William McKinney, who was buried on the Thursday. So many people wished to attend that it was deemed necessary to make it ticket-only for admission to the chapel in Creggan — chosen because it was the biggest church in the town. This meant that the traditional practice of burial out of a local parish church had to be abandoned in some cases.

Each family was allocated fifty tickets, a small number to go around. They were separated from each other in the chapel as there was no seating area designated for them. A side room was thoughtfully arranged for relatives who broke down during the Requiem Mass.

The Derry Journal reported that thirty thousand mourners stood outside the church in the rain, listening to the Mass over loudspeakers. Afterwards, privacy was impossible for the families. The scrutiny from the media and the public was hard to bear. The huge cortège moved off and, in the crowded confusion, it was hard for some of the relatives to know whether they were following the right coffin.

For years afterwards, some of the families were subjected to harassment by the Army and police. Often this meant house raids in the early hours. It was frightening, disruptive and time-consuming to be hauled out of bed, lined up and asked your name and age whilst soldiers or police went through your belongings.

The anger and shock was exacerbated when the British Government published its report into the event, by the Lord Chief Justice, Lord Widgery. His Tribunal of Inquiry produced a report on 18 April 1972 which was published after a mere eleven weeks. Widgery praised the actions of the Parachute Regiment and named some of the dead as gunmen and nail-bombers. As one relative said, it was as though his brother was murdered all over again. Edward (later Bishop) Daly, who was a curate in Derry and was present on Bloody Sunday, commented, 'What really made Bloody Sunday so obscene was that people after-wards, at the highest level of British justice, justified it.'[6]

One of Lord Widgery's omissions symbolises the inade-quacy and attitude of his Inquiry: he never visited the scene of the shootings nor did he walk the ground. A total of 582 statements were taken from eyewitnesses by local volun-teers from the Civil Rights Movement and the London-based National Council for Civil Liberties (NCCL), and these were offered to the Tribunal. Widgery accepted only fifteen of these statements and judged the forty soldiers who gave evidence to be more reliable. New evidence has since come to light of the involvement of other British Army regiments that were stationed in Derry at the time of Bloody Sunday — in particular, the Royal Anglians and the Light Air Defence Regiment who were stationed on the Derry Walls.

(A member of the Light Air Defence shot himself in the foot; he was the only soldier injured by gunfire that day.) It now appears certain that they, too, had joined in the firing on the marchers, but from different positions from the Paras — namely, the city walls. Had more of the eyewitness statements been taken into account at the time, this factor might have been given consideration by Widgery.[7]

It was to be another twenty years before the families of the dead felt able to campaign publicly on the issue (in the interim there had always been an annual commemorative march in Derry organised by Sinn Féin). After the twentieth anniversary, some of the relatives came together and launched the Bloody Sunday Justice Campaign with a view to having the whole event re-investigated — they wanted answers. Why had Bloody Sunday happened? Who had sanctioned the shooting dead and wounding of innocent civilians? Why had total war been visited on their community? They were convinced that Widgery's Report had been a cynical whitewash which excused the Army of any wrongdoing and contained a completely distorted and misleading account of events. Their aim was to clear the names of the dead, many of whom had been put on record in that official report as gunmen and nail-bombers.

For example, Linda Roddy's brother, William Nash, was found by Widgery to have had lead on his left hand, 'consistent with his having used a firearm'. However, William Nash was right-handed. In addition, his hands were not tested for lead until after his body had been picked up, most likely by the hands and feet, and thrown into the back of an army vehicle along with the bodies of John Young and Michael McDaid. Widgery concluded that ' ... [a]

very strong suspicion is raised that one or more' of those shot were using firearms.[8] Not one of the dead or injured was seen carrying a gun or bomb by any of the civilian eyewitnesses.

The families were seeking a fresh inquiry but it was to be a long struggle. It took six years of weekly meetings and hard campaigning to change public opinion and to harness crucial political support. Eventually, in early 1998, Tony Blair, the British Prime Minister, stood up in the House of Commons and announced the instigation of the Saville Inquiry. It was, he said, to investigate 'a definite matter of urgent public importance.... I believe it is in everybody's interests that the truth be established.' By setting up a second inquiry and effectively overturning the first, he made British legal history. The new Tribunal of Inquiry was to sit at the Guildhall, in Derry, and was headed by Lord Saville of Newdigate, an English Law Lord. There were two other judges appointed: Mr William Hoyt, the Chief Justice of the Canadian Province of New Brunswick, and Sir Edward Somers, a former judge of the Court of Appeal of New Zealand. The latter was subsequently replaced by an Australian, Mr John Toohey, a former Justice of the High Court of Australia.

Finally, in April 2000, after two years of preliminary evidence-gathering, the Inquiry began to hear evidence from eyewitnesses.

*

This book began, in early 1997, as a purely photographic project, originally intended as a series of portraits of people who had lost someone on Bloody Sunday.

The idea developed after I had been sitting on a train. I was reading a newspaper in which there was an eye-witness account of a man being shot to death one late January afternoon.[9] I remembered the story well — I had heard it from the man's father fifteen years before. No arrest had been made and the family had lived with his death, and the manner of his dying, for twenty-five years. For them there were no answers, no explanation, no blame. I wondered what had become of this grieving father. I remembered how he held up the corduroy jacket that his son was wearing on the day of his death and showed me the holes in the back. At the time I felt unable to take in fully what Jim Wray senior was telling me; his anger and grief hit me like a blast. Then, as I was sitting on the train, I read: 'Jim Wray fell close to the alleyway immobilised by a gunshot wound in the back.... To the horror of eyewitnesses, Wray was approached by a Para who shot him again in the back, at very close range. It was the execution of an already wounded man.'

As I thought about the Wrays, I found myself wondering what had become of the other families who had lost their sons or fathers so violently that day. I began to feel strongly that these people had been forgotten, their grief unacknowledged. How had they lived with their loss? With this in mind, I decided to ask each of them whether they would pose for a portrait, standing on the spot where their loved one had been shot.

I approached the work with some trepidation. I was aware that there would potentially be an issue of intrusion — would these people welcome the exposure to my camera of their private feelings? Would they be willing to bear witness after all this time? I also had personal concerns about the effect it might have on me to meet so many people connected with one horrific event. I began by making contact with family members who agreed to be photo-graphed. Later, I also met injured survivors and other eyewitnesses. I visualised the work as a series of portraits of people bearing witness to a past they could not forget.

It was a strange experience to walk around the familiar streets of the Bogside, now suddenly littered with unmarked killing grounds. For them, though, it was infinitely harder. Many had never been back to the actual place where their relative had been shot — had avoided it for twenty-five years. One woman felt like she was walking over her brother's grave. Another had disturbing flashbacks. Some of the portraits had to be done extremely quickly as the distress evoked was palpable.

As a photographer, I am usually quite animated with my subjects. However, when I started doing this series of portraits I was mostly silent, as they stood there on the spot, doing whatever they wanted on their occasion of remembrance.

When I first met some of the Bloody Sunday family members I was thinking about how their relatives had died, imagining the scene. But a comment by one of the first people I met, Raymond Wray — Jim Wray's brother — brought home to me the everyday family dimension of the tragedy. 'The chain has been broken by Jim's death,' he said. At the time of his death, Jim had been planning to get married and settle down. Raymond was mourning the loss of nieces and nephews he would never know.

I hadn't intended to conduct interviews, only to ask one simple question: What had they learned? But this very soon seemed hopelessly inadequate and I found myself swapping my notebook for a tape-recorder as I listened to the memories and stories. I wondered what the Bloody Sunday families could teach us about how people deal with shock and grief, how they contend with loss. It was striking that so many people were still around, living in the town after all these years. So often, after a mass killing, as in the former Yugoslavia for example, a community is scattered. In Derry it is still possible to talk to many relatives and eyewitnesses.

The sheer variety and wealth of perspectives that I encountered amongst those who spoke to me was what kept me working at times. Their language could be plain and poignant or sometimes complex with hurt.

Loss, terrible loss, was visited on the family of Jim Wray and those other thirteen families. Some people just never could deal with it; others negotiated a mutually supportive shouldering of the burden. Some left it to perhaps one or two family members to do the remembering and it was never discussed again. Some parents dealt with it through silence and apparent denial, out of fear that their other children would turn to the gun in anger and revenge. Grieving mothers and fathers often died young.

There was a loss of identity for the families as they became permanently associated with Bloody Sunday. They found themselves in a group apart; their privacy — a previous unselfconscious sense of themselves — became a thing of the past. This had the effect of separating them from everyone else in the town. Many people I spoke to made reference to this, and the words of Gerry Duddy, who lost his brother Jackie, reflect a widespread feeling:

Even now [after all these years], when I'm being introduced to people, I'm not Gerry Duddy who runs a football team, I'm Gerry Duddy whose brother was shot on Bloody Sunday. I need my own identity back, [it] makes me angry that I've lost it. At times I know it's the best way for people to explain who I am ... but it hurts. Am I not a person in my own right?

I still find it astonishing that the period in which the shootings occurred was so short. The term 'Bloody Sunday' evokes a day-long event. In fact, it lasted about 27 minutes, plus the time it had taken a little earlier in the afternoon to shoot Damien Donaghey and John Johnston. There seemed to be a terrible correlation between the tiny period of time it took to kill and injure, and the magnitude of its effect — on the community in Derry, on the history of the Troubles, on the political and historical relationship between Ireland and Britain, as well as on world opinion.

In the past thirty years of conflict in Northern Ireland some 3,500 people have died. Of those, some 357 people died at the hands of state forces. The worst year of all was 1972[10] and Bloody Sunday was the worst day of that year.

This book is not intended as a comprehensive account of what happened on the afternoon of 30 January 1972 nor as a definitive comment on Bloody Sunday's watershed status in recent Irish history. It is about the memories of those closest to the events of that day.

Notes to Introduction

1. Murray, Raymond, *State Violence in Northern Ireland*, Dublin: Mercier Press, 1998, p. 41.

2. Ó Dochertaigh, Niall, *From Civil Rights to Armalites*, Cork: Cork University Press, 1997, p. 309.

3. McClean, Raymond, *The Road to Bloody Sunday*, Derry: Guildhall Press, 1997, p. 74.

4. Memorandum from General Robert Ford, 'The Situation in Londonderry as at 7th January 1972', Saville Inquiry, doc. ref: Bundle 48.299-301.

5. Cashinella, Brian (*Sunday Times* journalist), Interview for *Sunday Bloody Sunday*, Channel 4, 30 January 1997.

6. Ibid.

7. Mullan, Don, *Eyewitness Bloody Sunday*, Dublin: Wolfhound Press, 1997.

8. Lord Widgery's Report, *Bloody Sunday 1972*, Uncovered Editions, Norwich: The Stationery Office, 2001, p 77.

9. Mullan, Don, Op. cit., quoted in *The Irish Times,* January 1997.

10. Rolston, Bill, *Unfinished Business: State Killings and the Quest for Truth*, Belfast: Beyond the Pale Publications, 2000, p. vii.

INTERVIEWS

CHARLES MORRISON

Charles Morrison was aged 26 on 30 January 1972. He was a steward on the Civil Rights march and was on the local Northern Ireland Civil Rights Association committee in Derry. He was also a member of the NICRA executive. At the time, he was working as a bricklayer and he subsequently erected the Bloody Sunday memorial statue in the Bogside, labouring through the night to ready it for the first anniversary. He now works as a City Inspector for Derry City Council. In 1998, he went to Namibia as an international observer, to monitor elections. He is still involved in community work and teaches Tai Chi in Derry.

I'd come back from England in 1968; my wife Kathleen and I were homeless; we got a place with a sink and a sofa-bed and we shared a toilet with at least forty other people.

At that time in Derry very few Catholics had houses — that's what the civil rights struggle was all about. But I've never seen civil rights as a purely Catholic issue; it's an all-embracing philosophy: at that time the Protestant working-class people in this city were just as badly treated as the Catholics. Bridget Bond was very active in the Derry Housing Action Committee and, in desperation, we asked her for help. And it was stunning what the lady did; she took us in and we stayed in her house for months until she got us a better place. An ordinary housewife, she worked in the factories in Derry; she had no academic training, but what a heart! I witnessed thousands of people she helped so unassumingly.

That's how I became involved in civil rights. I helped set up street committees in the Creggan area — when it was a no-go area — because there wasn't much service from the statutory agencies. We felt that people should share their skills; we had electricians, plumbers, nurses, someone to help fill out forms. It was about giving people ownership of their lives.

My wife Kathleen was very good with the sewing machine. She made the stewards' arm-bands and the banner for the march, which was later used to cover the body of Barney McGuigan. She hated where it ended up. We didn't think people were going to die.

I expected a big turn-out at the march because everybody was outraged about internment. It was striking that if you scanned around the march that day, you could see Sunday suits and ties — those were not people going out to be involved in riots. There were families from right across the whole social spectrum — rich people, the working class and the middle class — all marching together because it affected everybody, the introduction of this terrible legislation. After all the other injustices, it was very brutal and went into the very soul of the community. The British Army entered houses, threw children and mothers aside and took who they wanted. It was ridiculous because most of the people they were lifting were innocent — ordinary people who were then abused and tortured. Army intelligence was absolutely crazy. I had a friend who was arrested and taken to Ballykelly and he told me later that they stripped him naked and put a hessian bag over him. It was barbaric, they put him in overalls and cut out the crotch and dragged him over concrete, so his testicles were practically raw, and then they got a brush shaft and stuck it up his anus. Later he was awarded compensation for his injury.

The Civil Rights Movement was strictly non-violent; on Bloody Sunday we were confident with our stewarding of the march. We also knew that there would be no IRA activity in the Bogside. We made our protest in a peaceful and dignified manner until other people took other decisions. It wasn't about physically challenging the Government and the Army on the streets! I had no thought in my mind that the Army were going to enter the area and use live rounds. I felt guilty afterwards about having organised a march on which so many people died.

If we'd known, myself and the whole committee would not have proceeded. I was friends with the brothers and sisters of some of those who were killed. They're the most open-hearted people, and they wouldn't pass you in the street, for which I'm grateful. And at the Saville Inquiry recently, in his farewell statement, one of the barristers for the Army paid particular compliment to the relatives who were never once aggressive or unmannerly to him.

I was very close to the Army when they came into the Bogside; I saw a soldier drop down and fire from the hip and I remember pulling off my steward's arm-band because I thought I would be a target. Terrified, I ran into the courtyard at the back of the Rossville Flats and tried to get away through the entrance there. There were so many people it was like a cork, I couldn't get through. So I crawled on my knees down to the other entrance, but it was every bit as bad. At that stage I was in total confusion because the soldiers were all panning out as they were firing. I crawled back again to the first entrance and got out towards Joseph Place. People over at Free Derry Corner were shouting warnings — 'They're firing from the walls!' — so I crouched down for a long time under a walkway there.

One thing that haunts me, I would have physically assaulted somebody to get away. That's an awful emotion; I've thought about it often, and never want again to feel I would hurt another human being to save my own neck.

Eventually, I made my way up the Creggan up to Bridget's house. She was as white as a ghost. I didn't see Kathleen for maybe four hours or so afterwards, and didn't know if she was alive or dead.

I remember I didn't actually sleep for nearly two days. I was out taking statements for NICRA from the witnesses, and I felt I had to keep at it.* It was like a cloud descended on the town, and then you got the sense it was all over the island as well, from people who had come in to Derry. I was like a zombie at the funerals. It was the most outrageous day of rain, I remember that distinctly. Like everybody else, all I wanted was justice for the people. It's just indescribable, being in the middle of all the hurt and confusion. There was no need for a military machine to come in and mow down innocent people. You'd need to be a barbarian to take a decision to do a thing like that.

After the first few days of the Widgery Tribunal, when I saw Widgery arriving daily in an Army helicopter, I think my attitude was to mentally block it out. How could he be impartial? It was disgusting. How could he preside over such a set-up when there were so many people dead? For him to go home after that and get on with normal family life takes a cold heart. Widgery hurt an awful lot of people.

The hurt is still in the community. I don't know if the new Bloody Sunday inquiry will remove it; I think there are still forces in the establishment who'll never concede that decisions were made to do such a thing on Bloody Sunday, no matter how many millions come out of the public purse.

Afterwards, the whole political landscape changed. So many people in this country found themselves in

---

* There was a dispensary on Central Drive in Creggan and NICRA opened that up on behalf of the Committee for the Administration of Justice, from London, in order that statements could be taken from witnesses after Bloody Sunday.

a situation they didn't create, just by asking for fundamental human rights. Because of the violence surrounding the aftermath, the Northern Ireland Civil Rights Association (NICRA) didn't have a rôle any longer in terms of street protest. It would have been absolutely crazy to take people on the streets and so NICRA went into decline. Most of the work in which we were involved afterwards was housing, helping people to get benefits, and trying to get people jobs — fundamental community issues.

In a place like Derry, with high unemployment, you had young men and girls with so much energy. If they're caught up in political turmoil they have plenty of ways to spend it, and that's sad. Bad government creates very dangerous situations; they should be alert to this and give people a purpose to life. The amount of money that has been spent on security, bomb damage and compensation in this area over the last thirty years would have kept every person employed.

I'm so proud I was born in this city and so proud of its history. History is useless unless it is factual. In later years, when I decided to get myself educated, I studied Archaeology and History. I did my thesis on the Derry Walls — who constructed them and where the materials came from.

To this day I am still trying to get over Bloody Sunday. From the year 1972 I remember the march, I remember the funerals, I remember being involved in taking the statements of witnesses; no other day in the year 1972 can I recall. On reflection, it was probably the deep shock I was suffering. I'm so glad I didn't actually see people shot dead. I still have the same fire in my heart for justice; I think you're born with these great deep emotions — they never leave you.

Events like Bloody Sunday confirmed for me that there's a different way. When you put a gun in a man's hands and train him to kill, what do you expect him to do?

PATRICK McDAID

Patrick McDaid was 25 years old in 1972 and worked as a plumber. He was shot in the back on Bloody Sunday — in the circumstances, he had a lucky escape. He attended the Widgery Tribunal but was not asked to give evidence.

There was a bit of stone-throwing and suddenly everybody started running and shouting. I hadn't heard any shots. When I reached the top of Chamberlain Street, there were about four or five fellows carrying a woman who had been shot; I found out later she was Peggy Deery. They were having a bit of difficulty, so I helped them carry her [to one of the houses] ... we had to squeeze in ... there was that big a crowd. I said to myself the Brits will come and get us here, and I made my way back to the front door to look for help for Peggy Deery. Later, I heard they did lift everybody in there.

I got outside and there was a lot of gunfire. We were in a bad spot — the soldiers could come up the street behind us. I was panicking and about to move when a fellow ran out and fell. It was Jackie Duddy; he'd been shot. It scares you when you hear a fellow shot.

Myself and a few others got to the corner of the [Rossville] flats. A crowd was there already. The Army were shooting at everybody at the time, and they could have just come around the corner. Any other riot or trouble down the town, I could always stand and watch or make my way home. They were shooting people and I was trapped. That was the big difference.

The fellow ahead of me got away all right and I decided to make a run for it. I saw a wee wall and dived for cover. As I did, the soldiers fired. If I had been upright the bullet would have gone through me. A fellow landed behind me and said, 'They got you.' I didn't feel anything. He put his hand on my back and showed me blood. I panicked and I was still going to run towards Free Derry Corner. He grabbed me and said, 'Don't go that way, the Brits are down there.' So we made our way towards Joseph Place

and into the back door of the first house there. The amount of people in it was powerful. They took me upstairs to a bedroom and I lay on the floor on my stomach. I wouldn't lie on the bed because of the bleeding.

I lay there and, I remember well, they pulled up my jumper and somebody shouted, 'Get TCP!' I didn't know how bad I was, whether I was going to die or not. All I knew was that they were showing me blood all the time as they were cleaning the wound. When the ambulance came they put four or five of us into it. I didn't want to go but they closed the doors.

On the way over to the hospital, I said to the driver, 'That's dead on, you can leave me off here, I'll make my own way.' I was worried I would be arrested or get a beating if we were stopped by the Army. It wouldn't be the first time they stopped an ambulance and I didn't know what form those boys would be in.

At the hospital there was commotion — doctors and nurses all over the place. A fellow was lying on a trolley; I think he was dead. A doctor came to examine my back and asked, 'Where's the exit wound?' I hadn't the foggiest. Later, they took me up to theatre because I had a deep flesh wound and my backbone was visible. My family came up to see me. They didn't say much; I think they were relieved to find me sitting up in bed rather than lying in the morgue.

I was in hospital for two or three weeks — I can't remember exactly — I don't know how it affected me to be honest. It's just that some of the times when I'm at commemorations or marches I say to myself, I could be up there in the graveyard instead of walking along here; I was very lucky. Afterwards, I don't know what I did, it took me a

while to get back to normal. I went back to work. To this day a lot of people don't know I was shot on Bloody Sunday because I never spoke about it. I didn't want all the fuss. But I always stood by this Bloody Sunday crowd (the Bloody Sunday Justice Campaign) whatever they were doing.

It was mass murder. That fellow [Jackie Duddy] running past me had nothing in his hands. He made a break for it first and got killed. The paratroopers on the TV afterwards were saying they picked specific targets. I could be dead now and I'd have been classed a gunman. That split second I bent saved my life. I'll wait and see about the Inquiry. Are they going to call Widgery a liar or will they try to gloss over it? It's the British enquiring into themselves again.

LIAM WRAY

Jim Wray was 22 years old when he died. He was shot in the back as he ran away from the gunfire. According to eyewitnesses, Jim was finished off by a Para who stood over him as he lay wounded, and shot him in the back at close range. Jim had been working in England where he had met a young Israeli woman to whom he was engaged. Liam, his brother, was 18 years old in 1972. Liam also lost a close friend that day, Kevin McElhinney.

I went over to the hospital along with my uncle, at about half-six, to identify Jim. There were Paras outside and there were RUC inside. They were standing in the morgue with their guns and [they] searched us. They treated us very brusquely, saying nothing except, 'Go ahead'. I saw three bodies with tags on their toes just lying on the floor. Jim was lying on a trolley-bed against the wall and he was cold. I remember at the time trying to close his eyes, close his jaw. It was a very brutal occasion. It wasn't a respectful thing, there was no dignity about it.

I took three days off and when I went back to work I was a target of a lot of abuse. Many people from the 'other tradition' treated me like a leper or a terrorist because my brother was murdered. It was a strange year.

In 1971–1972, I really didn't believe that a soldier would shoot somebody who was unarmed. My eyes were brutally opened. The history books always say they were killed, as if it was something legitimate. It was murder and it should [be] on record as murder. If it isn't recognised for the injustice it was, the value of certain people's lives is zero. When you think that it was at government level, a decision so brutal so immoral....

Jim's death killed my mother. She was never the same after it. She was fifty when she died two years later; that devastated the family. Father refused to have anything to do with the Widgery Tribunal. He became extremely militant in the sense of 'burn everything British but their coal'.

Up to the start of the Civil Rights [Movement] and the Troubles in 1968–1969, we lived in Bishop Street, which was mixed. I had many friends who were Protestant. Once a year, you noticed a wee bit, coming up to the twelfth of August, they didn't play with you. When the troubles started we were very much in the front line. Our house was attacked in 1969 by loyalists. They tried to burn it down, and four others in the street. Shortly after that we moved to the Bogside. Because our house had been attacked by loyalists and the RUC and B Specials, my parents had no problem with me out defending the barricades with stones and bottles. The people in our area felt that the B Specials and the RUC were going to come in and shoot us down.

When the British Army came in August 1969, we saw them as saviours, coming in to defend us, we were under so much threat. It was a Thursday morning when the Army arrived; that evening my mother was out with a tray and tea in her best cups, with the best of what she could provide for them to eat. Within three weeks that changed, the police were back on the street, the army were standing beside them and firing gas and rubber bullets at us while the loyalist mobs cheered them on. Well, we were staunch civil-righters, make no mistake about it. But it wasn't that we were fighting for a United Ireland. My parents wouldn't have been pro-IRA or pro-violence. We wanted our civil rights, the vote, fair housing and equal opportunity.

That experience hardened us certainly — we became more interested in politics. As we lived in the Bog, we were a recipient of daily [CS] gassings by the British Army. When the gas got into the house, you just couldn't sit inside; it was really severe. I'd come home from work for my dinner and we'd have to eat it outside. There was gas in the street, but that was bearable.

We were turning towards the all-Ireland attitude. We saw it maybe as the answer to the problems we had, but we

LIAM WRAY (RIGHT) WITH HIS BROTHER, RAYMOND

weren't IRA supporters. So, when the Civil Rights march took off that day — it was such a massive march — it was the people's answer to internment: 'You are not going to brutalise us!' But they did and the end result was the murder of fourteen people.

The day after the funerals there was an open table at the end of Rossville Street where people were joining the Provisional IRA — that's how they became so strong. As open as that, hundreds were coming and putting their names down. I am not just on about teenagers, there were men in their twenties and early thirties.

At 18, it's very difficult looking at your relative in the coffin — that somebody could be so full of life and crack and all of a sudden it's not there, there's just a shell. And when you think about it — if you do think about it — you realise you wouldn't want anybody else to experience that ... you just didn't want to do it to anybody else. This was especially so for people that were the same age as the relative that died. But the people that don't have that close reality, they see the horrendous injustice and take up arms. I would have joined the IRA if Jim hadn't died on Bloody Sunday. Jim died and there is many a young man who decided from what he had seen that day that there is only one way to bring justice, and that's take up a gun. Now I'm not going to condemn the Provos — I don't feel I have the moral right. I say to myself, well, what option were those people left with, what was the experience they were taught?

There is hurt in all of these situations. I don't see myself as anything special. I'm aware the tragedy which struck our family has struck countless others throughout the communities in Northern Ireland. It has affected families in England. The difference is those families have had a respectful remembrance. Their government says what happened to them was murder. It's vitally important, that those who are responsible are brought to justice. Not because of vengeance but because if people feel that they can kill and walk away from it, be applauded and decorated for it,* then it will continue. If you do it once you'll do it again. There has been a lot of shoot-to-kill, a lot of Bloody Sundays in twos and threes and ones. You can't make political decisions that result in the murder of unarmed civilians.

It was easier for the relatives when we were campaigning: we had a clear goal, we had a great bond and we had control of the situation. Now [during the Saville Tribunal] we don't have control, but I feel we have a duty to those who died. It hurt to watch the lawyers for the Army protect the guilty, even though I know it is their job. I would like to walk away physically and emotionally. I am very tired, quite disillusioned, angry that the inhumanity of what happened has been lost in the legal arguments — that loving, vibrant people had their lives snatched away. I'm still grieving for my brother after thirty years, and for the calumny that was committed against him.

---

* Colonel Derek Wilford was later decorated.

JEAN HEGARTY

Jean is the sister of Kevin McElhinney who was 17 years old when he was shot as he tried to crawl to safety. He was pulled into a doorway of Rossville Flats and then carried up to the second-floor level where he died. Jean was 23 years old at the time and was living in Canada; she now lives in Ireland. Kevin was the middle child of five, and had worked in a shop up to the time of his death. After Kevin was killed, his mother washed his clothes over and over, trying to get the bloodstains out.

We heard the news about Bloody Sunday on the TV in Canada that afternoon. We knew there were people dead; my husband and I were both really worried about his younger brother. Then we kept thinking everything must be OK — we would have heard something. My parents didn't have a phone then so my aunt Eva phoned me on the Monday morning. When she rang that early, I knew instantly Kevin was dead. Then it was a panic trying to find the money to come home because we had moved into our first house on 4 December and were absolutely flat broke.

On the journey home, I remember talking to a woman on the plane. She was looking at her newspaper and saying, 'Isn't that terrible?' She obviously didn't realise who I was. It's funny, I don't think I responded much to her. There were pictures in the paper and I can remember thinking to myself, if the family hadn't told me ... if I had seen that newspaper, I don't know what I would have done.

When I think back on it now, it was nearly like being on drugs. I was looking on at all these events — they just didn't seem real. It almost seemed like I wasn't there. The trip home was just like being outside yourself looking on.

Kevin was a good bit younger than me. When I married and left Ireland he was fourteen. I arrived home and looked at the coffin and didn't know this young man. I remembered a pesky teenager. When I was courting he and our two sisters would have driven me mental. A person I didn't know had evolved during the time I was away and the opportunity to get to know him was gone. Nowadays the fact that I didn't know him hurts a lot. His friends knew him better than [I did]. Another thing: we all married and have our own children and he never got those opportunities.

When I got home, the house was constantly full of people. My mummy sent us with Mass cards to visit all the other families. I can vaguely recall going to the chapel up in Creggan and looking at all those coffins. That was the worst thing in the world, those coffins all in a row. The funeral was probably the most horrible day I ever remember. First of all, this having to fight your way into the church, it was upsetting. I remember being angry at the crowds. At the Mass I nearly cried, not for Kevin at all but for my daddy. I can remember looking at him across the aisle in the chapel. He just looked so beaten.

And then when we came outside ... I wasn't even sure if we were behind Kevin's coffin at one point because there was just so many people there. It was just unbelievable. It's strange how you can forget so much. I was worrying about my mother and the day even seemed to reflect the mood, so dark it was nearly like night in the cemetery. I can remember not being able to get too close to the grave at all because of the crowds. There were five families trying to bury someone in a very tight space.

After the funeral, I left. I went back to Canada and put Bloody Sunday behind me. I don't think I did it consciously. I didn't pay much attention to all the facts because I found it very, very painful. I know my parents' opinion was that Kevin was dead and nothing anybody did or said was going to change that. For them it wasn't a subject for discussion at all. My parents were never the same, never. But then, how could they be?

I had a difficult time dealing with the twenty-fifth anniversary. I got involved with the relatives' group [the Bloody Sunday Justice Campaign] in 1997 — after I came back from Canada — because I wanted to know what happened to Kevin. Until I read Don Mullan's book in 1997, I didn't know that they had taken him into the flats and that he died upstairs.

When the new Inquiry was announced, I was really optimistic [but] the longer it goes on, the less optimistic I am. While I wasn't expecting the Inquiry to be quick, the actual length of it is something I wasn't prepared for. I have some sympathy for the Inquiry team over the logistics which are a nightmare, but I would have liked both sides, the civilian and the Army evidence, to be heard as they went through each sector.* It's taken a long time to hear from the soldiers. Sometimes I wonder are they just doing it to wear us down.

Being there when Kevin's name is mentioned doesn't particularly upset me. But passing reference or comments provoke a bit more emotion in me than direct evidence. They catch me unaware. I am still hopeful that Kevin's name will be completely cleared and that people will understand that his actions were the actions of a 17-year-old trying to get away.

---

* The evidence at the Saville Inquiry is dealt with in geographical areas or sectors.

DAMIEN DONAGHEY

> Damien 'Bubbles' Donaghey was 15 years old on Bloody Sunday, and was the first person to be shot that day. He survived his injuries but his cousin, Gerard Donaghey, was killed. Damien had just left school and was about to start an apprenticeship. He was a keen and talented football player, but he could not continue with football or his trade because of his injury. He now works as a window-cleaner and is married with four children.

It was the last thing I expected. We were at a dance at the Stardust Room the night before. On the day, I was along with boys that I roamed about with and it was a happy march. We got to the bottom of William Street and we saw soldiers hidden in the bakery. There was a bit of stoning. They fired a rubber bullet which bounced off the wall and I went to get it. The next thing I knew, I was lying flat on my back, shot. Then, as Mr John Johnston was trying to lift me, they shot him.

Four or five people carried me into Mrs Shiels' house in Columbcille Court. Dr McClean came in and Fr Carolan. I was about 30 minutes lying there; they had to rip my trousers and put a tourniquet on me. Fr Carolan took me to hospital. As we drove past Harvey Street, we passed the Paras. I could see Colonel Wilford and General Ford giving interviews. There was a checkpoint on the bridge, and they flagged us down. But Fr Carolan just drove straight past — he was stopping for nobody. I think he knew at the time that there were others shot.

I had thought it was only myself and John Johnston. Then, when I was lying in Altnagelvin Hospital, Danny McGowan was brought in. He told me there were people shot, but he didn't say they were dead. We were moved out then, up to another ward. I didn't even know anybody was dead until the next day. It was unbelievable when I was told how many it was.

I was shot in the top part of my right leg. My femur was broken and later I had a big 6-inch steel pin through my knee; my leg was up in traction. I was six months on my back; a girl had to train me to walk again and I can only bend my leg 50 per cent even now. One of my legs is three-quarters of an inch shorter than the other. I have a limp still and arthritis in both knees. Lying in hospital was the worst of the whole lot. I was there for about eight or nine months altogether. I was the longest one in and was never as glad to get out of it. One consolation was a priest called Fr Tom O'Gara; he's dead now. He used to come and visit me and Peggy Deery. We were in the bones ward, Ward 6. And I had plenty of visitors; I think if you had nobody over to see you, it would send you mad. It was an open ward and any Brits that were shot were brought in and put down at the bottom end. At that time, they had two bodyguards watching them day and night.

I was 15 and had just finished school, and was trying to get a joinery apprenticeship. By the time I could walk right I was 19 and too old. I was left with no prospects and I ended up just a labourer. But I'm happily married, you know. I had to grow up quick. There were a lot of deaths in my family, with my mother and father when I was twelve; then my granny and my granddad, who had brought me up, died when I was not long out of hospital.

I [gave] my evidence at the new inquiry. It was a very nervous experience at the start. Then I said to myself, what have I to be worried about? I've done nothing wrong. Half-nine it started at and I was out before eleven o'clock. The Army lawyers got in touch beforehand to confirm they accepted I wasn't a nail-bomber. They were saying for years that we all had nail-bombs, guns, everything, and now they are saying we hadn't. So what's the use of spending millions and millions on the Tribunal?

The Ministry of Defence said in their opening state- ment to the Inquiry that there were thirty-four bodies of

IRA men who were killed on Bloody Sunday and then buried here and there. They say the soldiers who shot me also shot another boy who was an IRA nail-bomber. They're saying afterwards Johnny Johnston and I were taken into a house, but the other boy was popped in a hole! That's their excuse. The MoD are covering up but the truth will *have* to come out. Because at the end of it, it was the soldiers that did the killing, so Colonel Wilford and those boys have the responsibility. Wilford's going to be the fall guy, I think. They'd rather he was dead, so he couldn't be cross-examined. And the only time Edward Heath was asked about it he said he knew nothing. They will never put a former British Prime Minister down while he is still alive.

On the day [the soldiers] were able to do their damage, they weren't afraid, but they haven't got the guts to come here now. Will they tell the truth? In their statements they've lied and lied that much. Members of the Provisional IRA are all going to give their evidence, so why should the soldiers be afraid if they're telling the truth?

I think I was very lucky. I was left to tell my own story, but the poor people lying in the cemetery can't tell theirs at all.

MARGARET McGUIGAN

Margaret is Bernard McGuigan's daughter and is a baker by profession. She was 14 years old at the time of her father's death and was one of a family of six children, aged between 6 and 17. At great risk to his own life, Bernard had gone to comfort someone he did not even know. Paddy Doherty was lying injured and had been crying out in pain. Bernard was shot in the head whilst waving a white handkerchief. He died instantly.

RMS

It would have been around teatime on that Sunday when we heard that he was shot. I had gone around the corner to see if he was coming back up from the march and people had gathered [there]. They were saying that Barney McGuigan had been shot. I was taken then to my aunt's house. My mother got word that my father was shot in the foot. It wasn't until she actually got to Altnagelvin Hospital that she was told that he was dead.

The house never emptied from the start of the wake right up until the burial. Everything was sort of haphazard, there were people coming from everywhere.... We had a lot of reporters coming to the house, looking for statements. There are parts of it you do remember, parts of it you don't. We were totally numbed by the whole thing, it happened that quick. And my father being the type of person he was, he was the last person we would ever expect to get shot. It was a hard time too because it was my sister's birthday the day they were buried. Things were like a fog then for a long time.

His coffin was closed; we felt that we never got to say goodbye to him. There was no reality to it over the years and we never looked at photographs of the events until 1997. Seeing them in Don Mullan's book did bring the reality with it. Even that in itself was very hard especially with my Daddy's injuries. He had lost part of his face. To this day my mother still has not looked at the pictures. Every year the anniversary is very hard on her.

The January march is like having the funeral every year; because of the way they died, it's like we have never buried our dead. They were slighted on Bloody Sunday ... the truth didn't come out. Anywhere else in the world,

someone that went out to help someone would have been a hero, but Widgery implied my father was a gunman. We're still sitting in limbo; we want my father's name to be cleared so he can rest in peace. We are hoping for the best from the Saville Inquiry. Whatever they look into, we know that our people are innocent, we just want answers. It's very important that when I'm no longer here my children's children will be able to read the history books and know exactly what did happen; it is a big part of the history of this town. I am hoping and praying for the truth. Just to get that would change my life for me. My father has never got the honour he deserved.

All of my family have attended the Inquiry; it was very hard to hear my daddy's case being discussed because he is so important to us. One thing that came out in evidence, he was struck by a dum-dum bullet which was illegal issue. Forty shards of metal showed up in the x-ray of his head. What does that say? To me it was murder. His death brings fears with it because he went out and didn't come back. I have a time limit on my children when they go out and if they are not back I start to ring round — a panic sets in.

I don't really have any feelings towards the soldiers. We just want them to come forward and tell the truth. I couldn't say that I was bitter towards them; revenge doesn't come into it. My mother was very strong and she brought us up without hate or bitterness. The soldier that shot my father will have his God to meet one day and that will be his time to answer; it's out of our hands. That's the way I bring up my own children and I think it is the best way.

All the families that lost someone on that day have felt the same way about it: that there was great injustice done. There is a great strong link between the fourteen families. [My father] heard Paddy Doherty crying and he couldn't listen to him. The man needed somebody, that was my daddy's way of looking at it. He didn't know Paddy Doherty, he wouldn't have needed to know him. If anybody had been in trouble or hurt, he would have gone out to them. So that part of it didn't shock us — that was in his nature. We knew he would have done that.

It is terrible to miss someone for so long. He had so much vitality about him. I mean, he had so many friends, he was such a well-liked person. My father had no political views. He had as many Protestant friends as he had Catholic friends. That divide didn't even come into his own life. It was such a pity that he had to die the way he did.

ALANA BURKE

Alana Burke was injured on Bloody Sunday. Witnesses described seeing her being deliberately run down by an armoured personnel carrier and thrown some feet into the air. Her pelvis was damaged and her spine was fractured. At the time she was 18 years old and about to start a new job as an accounts clerk. She was an Ulster champion in Irish dancing. Her eldest son now attends university where he is studying Human Rights Law.

My mother and a few of my sisters were on the march that day. I lived in Bishop Street which wasn't far away from where everything was taking place. I remember it was bitterly cold but a lovely and bright sunny day. I was there with a friend, just a normal teen-ager out for the *craic* and to see who would be there, not thinking for a minute that something was going to happen. There was a bit of stone-throwing at the bottom of William Street and I was soaked right down to my underwear with dye by the water-cannons. Then I got sick from the CS gas. I remember vomiting in the street. People were beginning to get scared; I'd lost my friend and I wanted to go home. I took shelter in a house in Chamberlain Street for a while.

I was making my way home when there was the roar of the Saracens coming up at speed. Loads of people, maybe hundreds, were trying to get away. I caught on to some-body's tie and he pulled me along. Back then, everybody wore maxi coats — mine was made of heavy corduroy. I felt tired and sick and with the weight of my wet coat, my legs just wouldn't move. I remember being rooted to the spot in pure terror; looking behind me, I could see the Saracen coming. I thought, Jesus, I'm never going to get out of this, he's going to hit me. I just felt this awful thump and was crawling on all fours. After that, it's very, very confusing. Somebody picked me up and took me through an alleyway into one of the maisonettes in [Joseph Place].

I was lying flat on my back on the floor of this lady's living-room; there were a lot of women there and shoot-ing was going on outside. You could see directly out the window onto the forecourt. I remember one lady and she was shouting, 'Barney's gone out to see if he can help whoever is lying on the ground.' Everybody knew Barney (I knew him because he lived next door to my auntie in Creggan). She said, 'He'll be OK because he's got a handkerchief.' And the next thing they were all crying and shouting because he was shot. They just blew his brains out. Then I remember lying on the floor of the ambulance going to hospital; it was very crowded. Above me, on either side, were Barney McGuigan and Kevin McElhinney. I know now that they were both dead.

One of the vertebrae was crushed at the bottom of my spine and the nerves were damaged. I had no power at all in my legs for weeks. I felt withdrawn and didn't want to go out for months. I felt worthless and couldn't talk about it. The nightmares were awful. We were raided maybe once a week and I remember my mother crying at the hate mail from England. For years afterwards I felt guilty somehow that I survived when so many had been killed that day. I felt bad when I met the Wrays, for example. We all did Irish dancing together and were quite friendly. But their brother had been killed and I was still alive.

I went back to work after a couple of months, but I needed a walking stick. My injuries were mostly all down the right side. At the time, it didn't seem all that serious, but in years to come, I paid an enormous price.

When I got married, I had a child by Caesarean because my pelvis was crushed. Little did I know that was going to be the one and only time because, after Gareth was born, I never seemed to pick up, I seemed to be sick all the time. When I was 30, I had a bout of tuberculosis for

eighteen months and was put into isolation which meant no contact with my family, no affection and touching. I've had five operations — they took ovaries, tubes and eventually the womb. I still take painkillers, very strong ones.

Suddenly, about two-and-a-half years ago, one Sunday, I couldn't move my legs. My husband, Michael, took me to hospital and I saw the orthopaedic surgeon who came with an x-ray that he had dug up from somewhere. 'Do you realise that you have a massive fracture in the bottom of your spine and it's been there a long, long time,' he says. 'And that's why you're losing the power of your legs.' And that's the first I knew of it. He says there's nothing they can do.

It was a terrible day for everybody in Derry, but it dictated the whole outcome of my life. That day decided my fate.

ITA McKINNEY &
REGINA McKINNEY

Ita was 33 years old when she was widowed on Bloody Sunday. She had seven children and gave birth to her eighth one week after her husband's death. She named the baby Gerald, after her husband, but could not call him by his name for years. Gerald McKinney had his own metalwork business. He loved roller-skating and football. He died at the age of 35 when he went to help Gerard Donaghey. Afterwards, Ita lost so much weight that she had to wear children's clothes.

Regina is the daughter of Gerald and Ita McKinney.

Ita McKinney

We were watching the news that Sunday, me and the young ones, and they gave out that there were four shot. When I found out Gerry was dead, I was shocked; it lasted for years. I know I went funny every year. I just went into myself; I was bad tempered and I locked myself in the bedroom. I was depressed. It would last for three months or so. I don't really know why it changed around the twentieth anniversary — maybe it was just time. I think about Gerry every day. What can you do? You have to go on. He was great, he was beautiful. Aye, in my eyes, he was beautiful. I often wonder what he would look like now after thirty years.

He was brave, he went out to the wee boy, Gerard Donaghey. But I wasn't brave. I wouldn't go out for years. I wouldn't go down the town; that's why I don't know half of Derry. Everybody did the shopping for me, all the girls. I never went out and any time that I did, there was shooting or bombs and that put the heart out of me then again.

Definitely, I would like to see my husband's name cleared, that's the most important thing. I'd like to see them all cleared — sure they were innocent anyway.

Regina McKinney

I was 8 when my daddy died, I never actually got to see him. It affects the rest of your life when you don't get to say goodbye. I used to think, well, I never saw him to say cheerio. As a child, I thought he could just be away somewhere.

I never told anybody he was dead because I couldn't bear to be the only one without a daddy. I told them at school he was in Dublin and that he'd be home for the weekend until I got found out. I was about 12 years old. Some of them in my class thought I was being silly. When I was 23, I went to a priest and he said I needed counselling. I turned to God for everything in my life and started the healing process.

And I think you have to forgive, so I dealt with forgiveness of soldiers and it healed me too. Because if you have bitterness within yourself, you are hurting yourself and nobody else. I wouldn't want a soldier to be killed or anything just because my daddy was shot. I forgive whoever did it. At the end of the day, we don't know how that soldier, or any other soldier, felt through all these years. God is the judge of everybody and he'll judge me as he will judge the soldier that pulled the trigger.

There were always memories, it totally affects your life. Also, we have watched my mummy get depressed all those years at a certain time — 'round about November; it lasted into March or April — then she would start coming out of the feelings. This went on for twenty years.

It's heartbreaking that my daddy was not there to see us getting married, or for some of us, our first communion. You wonder what would he have been like as a grandda. There are times you'd love just to talk to him. He's not there, it's like something stolen. That's what it was, he was stolen away.

The twenty-fifth anniversary was the hardest. I had a week of nightmares after seeing Barney McGuigan's

ITA McKINNEY (RIGHT) AND REGINA McKINNEY

picture in the front of the paper; every single night I was up crying, dreaming somebody was getting killed again. Everything came back, things that you wouldn't have been aware of as children.

I am quite anxious about the Saville Inquiry — it opens up the wound again. It's a family thing: we would want to know what really happened. It's our place to know about my daddy. But we are scared to hear the truth, how he died.

I would like them to admit that they are wrong, but going by the general behaviour of the British Government, it would be hard for them to show themselves up for what they did. It would speak volumes to the world if they took stock and admitted that they were in the wrong, if they apologised with no ifs or buts.

It's hard not to be angry which is why I don't want to get caught up in the whole Inquiry. I think we'll get more justice for my daddy from believing and praying that it will come all right. To me, the truth will always come out eventually — it can't stay hidden forever. Our loved ones are not only a name, they are lots of things.

They haven't just killed a father, they have killed a grandfather and a father-in-law too.

FLOYD GILMOUR

Hugh Gilmour, the youngest of eight children, was 17 years old when he was shot. He worked as a tyre-fitter and went to the cinema every Friday night with a group of friends. He also loved football and supported the Liverpool team. He had bought his first car and was learning to drive at the time of Bloody Sunday. Hugh was shot in the arm. Then, it seems that he was shot a second time whilst running for home. He died at the entrance to the Rossville Flats. His brother, Floyd, was 24 years old at the time. A strong supporter of the Bloody Sunday Justice Campaign, Floyd died of cancer in May 2001.

His widow, Anna, adds: 'His greatest wish was to see true justice not only for Hugh, but for all those who suffered as a result of Bloody Sunday.'

My brother-in-law came to the door and said that Hugh had been shot dead and was lying at the front of the flats. Confusion broke out. My parents and sisters were roaring and crying. I was trying to cope with this news and hold my mother and sisters back from rushing out. We couldn't get to him because the shooting was still going on. If I hadn't done that, they could have been shot too. We weren't able to reach Hugh before the ambulance took him away. When we did get out to look for him, Barney McGuigan was still lying there — oh, it was terrible, that. I knew Barney personally for years, and I saw him lying there with the head just blown clean off him. You wouldn't have known him, he was that badly shot.

We went over to the hospital, still hoping against hope that it wasn't true because we hadn't seen Hugh then. I didn't go into the morgue to identify the body — my brother and sister went in. They said afterwards there were so many there, and they had to go around them all. He was the very last. They knew him by his hands before they even lifted the sheet because he worked in the tyre company and his nails were usually black.

I remember the day twenty-five years ago, I remember everything. My mother and father have died since, and you accept a natural death. Whereas, twenty-five years on, I still can't accept Hugh dying. It should not have happened. It was terrible. He was 17 and, being the youngest and the only one left in the house, it made things doubly hard. If anything, it made it harder to live with than people might realise. My mother, even until she died — which was sixteen years after the event — would still sit and cry. It just broke her heart — the day that they shot my brother, they killed her. She was still there for us, but within herself she just died. We convinced her to move house. For her to get to the shops she would have to keep passing the spot were Hugh lay, you see.

The whole of the city was stunned. You could feel it, you could see it. There was a stunned silence for almost a week afterwards. People were walking about in a trance. There was nothing else being spoken about. So you can imagine the atmosphere about the place — a terrible time, a terrible time. It's a time that has not gone away for anybody, never mind just the families. Those who were there saw horrific things — people with their hands in the air being shot in front of them for no reason. They were shot like animals.

My own brother was running towards the flats, there are photos of him running and being shot. He was hit in the left arm and it went right through him and came out the other arm. How those people aren't haunted is beyond me. They know, as we know, that they shot innocent people that day.

MICHAEL BRADLEY

Michael Bradley was 22 years old when he was shot and was injured in both arms and the abdomen. Initially in hospital for three months, he needed both skin and bone grafts. He took an active interest in music, playing in an accordion band, and had just finished his painting and decorating apprenticeship. However, having lost the use of his right hand, he never practised his trade.

Everyone was running. I made my way towards the Rossville Flats and stopped to catch my breath when a lady came running past and said, 'Look son, you'd better not stay here, they're shooting live bullets out there, there's a young man lying dead.' Curiosity got the better of me and I went back into the forecourt of the Rossville Flats. People were still running in every direction, trying to get away. I saw two [Army] personnel carriers, and soldiers jumping out of them. They just took up positions out in the open. They weren't trying to hide themselves. All of a sudden, I spotted a young boy lying — there was a group of protesters around him. I realised it was Jackie Duddy, a friend of mine; we both came from Creggan Heights. I shouted over to the soldiers, really bitter, 'Come on, you hateful bastards; come on, fucking shoot me!' All of a sudden, I felt this merciful heavy thud and I thought, Jesus, what hit me? I threw my left arm over my right forearm, thinking I had been hit by a rubber bullet.

Within seconds, the blood came gushing down through my fingers. I didn't realise I also had a bullet through my left arm and one through my stomach. I didn't pass out. I still had my legs so I clambered back over a little wall. I don't know whether I reached the corner, but when I woke up I was in a house in Joseph Place.

I was lying in a hallway. All I could hear was, 'Get a priest, get an ambulance man.' I could see heads looking down at me. A young priest was brought to me, Fr Thomas O'Gara. He knelt down, put my head on his knees and gave me the last rites. Next to come was the first-aid man, Noel McCloone. I could smell my flesh burning, my abdomen was stinging. I asked for a drink, my mouth was so dry. As the first-aid man lifted my jumper, I saw him nodding to the priest as if to say 'No'. I thought, what's going on? I thought of my wife who was expecting our first baby — we had only been married nine months. I was panicking and kept asking, 'Am I going to die, Father?' Someone wet my lips with a flannel.

An ambulance had drawn up outside and I was carried out. I could hear shooting. Another priest, Fr Mulvey, came waving a white handkerchief. He shouted to the soldiers at the barricade, 'Hold your fire till we get this man into the ambulance'. A body was placed in the ambulance and then a second one. It was Paddy Doherty and young Hugh Gilmour, I was sure that this was a death ambulance. I was shivering and I remember well that Fr O'Gara tucked a blanket around me. He was chewing some gum and he said to me, 'Mickey, I wish I had some more of this gum. I'd love to give you a piece.' He kept talking to me. Looking back, I realise that this gentle young priest was trying to distract me. I made him promise that he wouldn't leave my side and he didn't.

The hospital entrance was lined with police and soldiers. There were rumours flying around that the Army and the police were waiting for the bodies of the dead and injured so they could contaminate them. They wanted evidence that people were carrying firearms or bombs. This was on my mind, so I decided that the first person that came near me would get a size-nine boot. The nurses and doctors were keeping them back as much as they could. I panicked as they lifted me from the ambulance and kicked out as a nurse tried to put a cardboard tag on my foot. Unfortunately, she went flying up the

corridor. Fr O'Gara was trying to calm me. Inside, two nurses stood looking in amazement. I was cold and shivering they didn't know what to do because all they saw was blood.

I said, 'Look kids, my bottom half is clear. It's all on my top half.' I was stammering away and, as they were cutting the clothes off me, I heard a voice from the other side of the curtain. It was Peggy Deery* who lived in Creggan Heights too. She was shot — I didn't realise at the time how bad she was, she said she was all right. Then, in walked the surgeon, George Fenton, a big gentleman dressed in white — 'Get that man straight to theatre.' I'll never forget looking above me at the sign as we went into the operating area, 'Booties must be worn beyond this point.' Fr O'Gara said, 'I'll be waiting for you.' I was told afterwards, had the bullet in my abdomen been an inch to the left, I'd have been in the morgue.

What I'll never forget about the experience was the wing we were in had soldiers in it — British soldiers. This young girl, she was a military police woman, she kept walking around in the corridor and looking in. I said to one of the nurses, 'Tell the military policewoman that if she wants to come in here and talk to me, that's OK.' She came in and sat on my bed, she was almost in tears, and says, 'Look, sir, I know how you feel, you feel angry.' And I said, 'No, love, you don't know how I feel. As long as it wasn't you that pulled the trigger, then I have no animosity towards you.'

I still can't believe that they came to kill us — not to maim, but to kill. The MoD are now doing a Pontious-Pilate act and washing their hands of the young soldiers, but there's still officers out there now with their heads high, saying their men did a good job. I don't care what Wilford says, that man came into this town to murder.

---

* Peggy Deery was the only woman shot that day. The other woman injured, Alana Burke, was run over by a British Army vehicle.

ALICE LONG

Alice Long was 18 years old in 1972 and was working as a shirt-maker. She had been a volunteer first-aider since the age of 10. She came under fire a number of times on Bloody Sunday and the Pope later awarded her a medal for bravery. Together with fourteen of her colleagues from the Knights of Malta, Alice offered evidence to the Widgery Tribunal, but this was rejected.

It was like cowboys opening fire. Some had the rifles down at their hips. They were out and determined to kill, and anybody that escaped that day was very lucky.

About four o'clock we got the first casualty, a wee girl overcome with gas. Then I went to the Shiels' house where there were two shot. Johnny Johnston kept insisting it was all right — he didn't realise how bad he was. Damien Donaghey had been shot in the leg, and we put a tourniquet on him.

I met Leo Day, our superior officer. Someone told us that there were three young fellows shot and put into a Saracen tank in Rossville Street. We could hear shooting as we went over with our hands up and asked if we could see who was inside. Fr Mulvey was there and he said, 'They'll not let me in to give the last rites.' The door was ajar. Leo Day and I looked in. There were three fellows piled on top of each other, all face downwards with their coats pulled over their heads. We heard a slight moan. I went to open the door of the Saracen but the soldier standing there kicked it shut. He was very wee and had on a different uniform from the rest of the Paras — no markings or insignia, and a different scarf too. Leo and I saw a foot twitch, so I tried once more, and he kicked it shut again. There was a bit of an argument with him and he pulled up his gun and poked it into a small side flap on the Saracen — he had to reach right up — and he said, 'When we do this, we do it right. The Parachute Regiment doesn't make mistakes.' Then he fired into the tank and said, 'Well that's the end of them Fenian bastards.'

I lifted two bullet cases off the ground. Fr Mulvey was saying they were shooting dum-dum bullets — if you get a chance, pick them up. They were cut wide open at one end like a flower with petals. I put [the cases] in my pocket but the soldier saw and cocked his gun at me, so I had to leave them. While I was standing there, a shot came out of the blue, I don't know in what direction. I don't think it was meant for me because it just skimmed my coat and left a burn mark.

I went over to the Rossville Flats where I saw Barney McGuigan lying dead. They were still shooting so I took cover for a few minutes. We had to try to get ambulances. So myself and Antoinette Coyle, another Knight of Malta, walked down Chamberlain Street, in the direction of the firing. I was very afraid as I went down the centre of the road with my hands in the air. Only for my white uniform coat, they didn't do anything.

I told the Army that I needed ambulances for the injured. One of the soldiers laughed and said, 'Why do you need ambulances? The Paras shoot to kill, not maim.' They sent me off in the wrong direction. As I came running back, the shooting had stopped. I heard them making jokes, 'How many did you get?' And how they were going to celebrate that night. Some officer was shouting, 'Well done, boys. Well done!'

It took perhaps 30 minutes for the ambulances to arrive. Apparently, they had been stopped by the Army. It was all happening that quick when they came because the Army were still firing. I had to dive for cover at one point. A little later we were in the last ambulance with someone who had died, Fr Mulvey had just given him the last rites … the firing started again, and we both had to lie down on the floor of the ambulance for cover.

I hardly treated anyone that day because they were all dead. I was in a trance the whole walk home. When I got in, I started crying. The Army withheld all experienced medical help. We could only do so much — we didn't have the right equipment — but at least we tried to ease the pain for whoever we could. The shock really hit me that night and the next day. Afterwards, I promised myself that I was going to lose all memory of it, and worked hard at trying to forget. I had nightmares for a couple of months; throughout the years they gradually wore off. It took a long time.

I gave evidence at the Bloody Sunday Inquiry, to help the families of the dead, but I don't believe that the British will give justice; they'll do everything to twist it, they'll pull every legal wrangle that they can. Words will not explain how I feel — some of those fellows were just my age and they were getting shot down for no reason.

LINDA RODDY

William Nash, Linda's brother, was 19 years old when he died. He was shot and fell almost on top of Michael McDaid and John Young. Linda was aged 13 at the time. There were thirteen children in their family, and William was the middle child. He left school at 15 and got a job as a messenger boy. At the time of his death, he was employed as a dock worker. After his death, the Army said that they found lead on his left hand from firing a gun. However, William was right-handed.

William was very humorous, he was the joker of the pack, always smiling. You miss somebody like that out of the house — the laughter is gone with him. He was hardworking and generous with his money. After work, he did judo or played table tennis. Sport was very important in my family — my brother Charlie fought for the world title and boxed in the 1972 Munich Olympic Games. William loved country-and-western music. Because he was so tall the kids on the street called him 'Tarzan'. He was very fond of children. They would always follow him to get up on his shoulders.

My father watched William fall and went to him at the barricade. They were both on that march that day because they believed that internment was wrong. He waved, screamed to the paratroopers, 'This is my son, this is my son. I need help!' One of the officers shot him in the arm. You don't do that to a dog. Then they dragged my brother's body away and his possessions were stolen: a graduation ring, his chain and cross, and his money. My father was left in shock to get first aid for himself.

Normally, when a person dies, you're told what happened, you grieve and get on with the rest of your life. I have been lied to for thirty years — it's hard to take. Legally, it's still on the record that William was a gunman. The British Army will not take responsibility for his murder. People do not realise the heartache that this Inquiry has caused the families. Being taken back to 1972 is very painful. My brother Paddy has had to stop attending because it's affecting his health both mentally and physically. The outcome we want from Saville is the exoneration of the dead and wounded. The Widgery Report should be officially discredited and the soldiers who did the shooting prosecuted.

My mother was in Altnagelvin Hospital at the time of Bloody Sunday, after a major heart attack. The doctor didn't let her know until the day of the funeral. They heavily sedated her and wheeled my father down from his ward. He said it was the hardest thing he ever had to do. Afterwards, he drank non-stop for two years — that's the way he dealt with it. Maybe not the best way, but the only way at the time. Because of Don Mullan's book and the eyewitness statements, we discovered that my brother lived for 5–10 minutes. That was hard to take. When I told my father what I had discovered, he said, 'How could I have ever told your mother?' It was better that she thought that he died instantly.

My other brother got married the day before [Bloody Sunday]; we had a wonderful day although it was a bit emotional because my mother wasn't there. To go from that, to the next day, to a wake, it was too hard to take. I was a very confused 13-year-old. I found the funerals terrible. Both of my parents were in hospital, but I believed that when they came home they would help me understand what was happening. And things would be OK again. But after Bloody Sunday, neither of them wanted to live. My mother had given up and I couldn't do any thing; all she had to do to live was eat but she wouldn't. Did you ever know when you looked at somebody's face that things were the way they were? She died in 1979. My father was traumatised, and coming up to the anniversaries his mind was hell. He thought everybody was a Paratrooper and that they were out to kill him. It was terrible to watch. He died in 1999.

The British Army gave my family special attention afterwards — house-raids, harassment, abuse. We were getting hate mail from God knows where. In one week I remember eight raids. I grew up believing that my brother must have been a gunman because why else would we be treated this way? I believed it until I was 18. I was arrested a few times and physically abused in front of many people. Every time I saw a foot patrol, I ran. From the age of 13 until 19 it was the only way I could survive. I became an expert at running. The army expected the families to look for revenge and tried to break our spirits. Revenge was never an option because of how we were brought up.

I got a phone call from a soldier, I don't know if it was the boy that murdered my brother. He was telling me, 'I'm very sorry, please forgive me.' But how do you deal with phone calls like that? I have no reason to believe it was a prank. I did trace the call and I know where it came from. I have a feeling he definitely was here on Bloody Sunday. He was remorseful, but if somebody is going to call me then they have to tell me for what exactly they want forgiveness. He was very distressed and there was absolutely nothing I could do to help him. I didn't have the opportunity to say to him, if you are genuinely sorry and if you can forgive yourself and God can forgive you, then who am I? I'm not important. What I want to do is just get on with my life. He should get on with his. He may have a family and for them he needs to be a healthy person again.

It was the first time I experienced death. I still can't walk along the street where he was murdered without my eyes being fixated on that particular spot.

DANIEL GILLESPIE

Because he did not seek hospital treatment, Daniel Gillespie was not included in the official list of Bloody Sunday wounded. He was 32 years old at the time, and had been married for ten years, to Frances. They had four children and lived in the Bogside. Frances was standing at the garden gate, their youngest in her arms, listening to the shooting, when Daniel was helped up the street; he was bleeding profusely. He had a very narrow escape — a bullet grazed his head, leaving a permanent groove in his skull.

I was right down at the front near the barricade in William Street with a friend. The rubber and the gas started flying. I saw a rubber bullet coming and side-stepped. A fellow called Worsky got it slap on the mouth. It had a slit with glass in it. By that time it was getting a bit rough, so we headed off and I left my friend near the entrance into the High Flats.* Being nosy, I drifted back to see what was going on. I saw the Saracen that pinned Alana Burke against the wall. It came tearing madly down — the dust and the dirt were flying. I said, 'There has to be somebody dead there,' and I started to run. The Paras were jumping out; I heard shooting behind me.

The next thing was a wee blond-haired young fellow, Michael Kelly, getting carried shoulder-height. I saw the life going out of him. I got into Glenfada Park and there were young fellows breaking slabs of concrete. I said to them, 'Look, boys, it's live rounds they're firing.' At that, a Brit came through, pointing a gun. I heard a 'whack' and I went down. When I started to come round, there was a terrible stinging, burning sensation. I thought my head was going to burst. The young fellows — one on each side of me — said, 'Are you all right, mister?' There was another shot; all I heard was a grunt and a body fell on top of me. I didn't look round. I pushed him off me and ran for my life.

There was somebody calling, 'Come on in here, mister,' but I kept going. I remember a woman shouting, 'There's a man with the top of his head blown off!' I was feeling for a hole in my head, the blood was that thick on me, it was like liver. I felt very dazed, I made a bee-line for home and fell twice on the steps coming out of Glenfada [Park].

I was leaning against a wall, shaking, when Joe Mahon and Michael Canavan came along and brought me over the street to the house. Frances was standing at the gate; she had the wee one in her arms, Anne — she was only about eighteen months. There was so much blood it was stinging my eyes. Michael said, 'Have you got a face cloth or something to see who this fella is?' She said, 'That's my husband.'

They took me down to Vinny Coyle's house at the corner. It was just like a first-aid camp; people affected by the CS gas were taken in there too. 'Tell me where I'm shot,' I remember saying. They said, 'There's a groove there, you'll have to get that stitched.' I said, 'No, just cut the hair and put Cicatrin** powder on it.' I got some plasters and that was it. I was lucky that I had a blue woollen hat on which Frances had knitted. Without the hat, I'd be worm food. It had tears through it where the bullet ripped it.

That evening, I had to go over to the morgue because I thought my brother was shot. I was reluctant to go — there was a rumour that people were getting arrested going to the hospital. The police were standing outside the morgue in the dark, singing a song from the Coke advert: 'I'd like to Teach the World to Sing'.

Directly I went inside [the morgue], I saw a young fellow with long black hair, a white flannel blanket over him and black socks with a big hole in the heel — it was Jackie Duddy. There were other bodies covered in blankets on the floor. A detective spoke to me and I said, 'Just fuck off!' I

---

* The High Flats was a local term for the Rossville Flats.
** An antiseptic powder.

have a bad tongue at times. Then a medic came over saying, 'Come on up here.' We went up the other end and I looked at a body. 'Jesus, I'm not too sure,' and he said, 'Well, how would you know?' I said, 'He had a tooth capped on Friday.' He lifted the lip — it wasn't my brother, the tooth wasn't capped.

A couple of days later a knock came on the front door, this hoity-toity fellow was asking, 'Were you shot on Sunday in Glenfada Park? Could you tell me where the gunman was standing?' He was no journalist. Normally, they'd come with and pen and paper or something in their hand. I gave him such a slap that I put him over my gate. He took flight.

I was so shattered I couldn't go to the funerals. For a long time I was very nervous.... I ate valium for a couple of years; I'm still on them.

I wouldn't go to a march afterwards. I always have the dread that somebody foolhardy was going to step out with a gun and there would be more dead. I never talked about it — none of my children knew about me getting shot. If it came on the TV, I'd have nightmares. When I gave an interview in 1996, it brought it all back. I was hospitalised with a nose haemorrhage; my blood pressure was sky high. Afterwards, I was jumping up in my sleep, shouting, 'I'm shot! I'm dead!'

I had an old Morris Minor van and did a bit of removal work. I think that's what kept me going, getting the odd pound here and there. Through CB radio, I dabbled around and studied for my amateur radio licence. I kept birds too.

If I met the soldier who shot me, I'd ask him, 'Why?' Because I had nothing in my hand. They didn't come in with their faces blackened for nothing. It's a sad excuse for the Army to say they were shooting at gunmen. If the IRA were there that day, it would have been a turkey-shoot for them with the Army out in the open.

BETTY WALKER & MICHELLE WALKER

Betty's brother, Michael McDaid, was 20 years old when he died at the rubble barricade on Rossville Street. The second youngest of twelve children, he was affectionate and enjoyed playing with his nieces and nephews most Sunday mornings. In the afternoon, he and his mother would take a drive in the car they had bought together. Betty was 25 when Michael died.

Michelle is Betty's daughter. She was 3 years old in 1972.

Betty Walker

At the time, I was in Wales as my husband was in the RAF. We waited until one o'clock in the morning for news. When I got home on the Monday night, Michael's body was already there in the coffin. My brother stood behind me and told me to put my hand on his face so I could feel the indentation. It was well packed, you wouldn't have known that's where he was shot. There were twelve of us. After my brother's murder, I never heard my mother mention his name. They say that you can get over your husband's death but never your child's. All these years of not talking about it.... I couldn't carry that.

Michael left school at fifteen and worked for a year or two in Bradley's shop, until he came of age, and then they took him into the bar. That was his life — he absolutely loved it and, on the day of the march, his boss didn't want him to go because a lot of people apparently said there'd be trouble.

Now, he was a young man, well-dressed. He never wore jeans; when he went to work at the bar in the morning, he had a shirt and tie on. In the afternoon, he had a few hours off. He would have had a shower, put on clean clothes — shirt and tie — and back to work again. A car, that was his greatest ambition and he got it. He was fantastic — everybody in this area knew him — he wouldn't have passed anybody without saying hello. There's a lot of elderly ladies lived across between where he was born and the street where he worked, and every one of them knew him.

There was a time after Michael's death that I hated every thing English. If a soldier was killed, I used to say,

'So? He was well paid, he was trained for what he was doing.' But no, he was somebody's son too — that's the way I feel now; I don't have the bitterness any more that I used to have. What changed that was my own children. Life changes when you realise that you could lose one of your own. If the soldier that shot my brother told me he was sorry, I would ask him why he had done it. The hatred: maybe not everybody can deal with it, but it has certainly left me.

Until Don Mullan's book, we took it for granted that Michael was shot by soldiers at ground level. Now it seems he was one of the three young men who was hit by an Army sniper on the Derry walls overlooking the Bogside. When you know that they were innocent and that the British Government — the next day — labelled them gunmen, it's very hard to live with. After that, because of Michael and the other thirteen that were killed, the youngsters lined up in their thousands to join the IRA. A whole lot of them died for it, many spent a lifetime in jail and a lot of them were destroyed.

This Lord Saville may seem nice on the television, but he's a member of the British Establishment so how can he and the other two men with him sit there and be impartial? At the end of the day, I don't need the British Government to tell me that my brother was innocent.

Michelle Walker

From day one, the truth was totally covered up by propaganda. This past year there's light been brought into it and justice has to come out of it, especially for my

BETTY WALKER (RIGHT) AND MICHELLE WALKER

mammy and her brothers and sisters. If my granny was living now, she couldn't cope with this. It was cold-blooded murder. But my generation, I think we're totally sick of it. We're used to the way Bloody Sunday has been treated. It has been really sad. I think the British are going to be left in the position where they can't but apologise for it because there's been so much new evidence.

I don't remember Bloody Sunday itself but I remember lying in bed at night, soldiers coming into the house. My sister and I shared a bedroom and we had a doll's house. I remember soldiers coming in and smashing it and pulling the dolls apart. But, as a Christian, when I look now at the police and soldiers, I think there is a lot of brainwashing that goes on. There is hatred that has to be changed from within themselves. I don't feel hatred for them, don't want to feel that way. I've seen too much of it. During the Troubles it was normal to see terrible things. I was talking to someone who told me that when he was a child his best friend was blown up in front of him down in the Bogside. He was eating a bag of chips at the time and he went on eating the chips. I've had friends killed and blown up — I don't want that any more. For myself, I need to be able to forgive and get on with life.

I've had customers come into the salon who were witnesses at the Inquiry. One lady who was in having her hair done was really upset. She was made out to be a liar on the stand. All she was doing, for the first time in thirty years, was sharing what she had seen looking out of her window in Glenfada Park. She thought, what way is that to get at the truth of anything? Badgering people and saying they didn't see what they did? Where's the justice in that?

I look at my mammy and John Kelly and the rest of them and, thirty years on, that hurt hasn't gone yet. Honest to God, if it is going to be sorted out, let it be soon.

Dr Raymond McClean

Dr McClean has been a doctor in Derry for nearly forty years and was present on Bloody Sunday. While working as a GP during the Troubles, he researched the harmful effects of heavy exposure to CS gas on the population in Derry. He discusses this subject in his book, The Road to Bloody Sunday *(Guildhall Press, Derry, 1983, revised 1997). As a member of the SDLP, he was elected Mayor of Derry in 1973. He was the first nationalist to hold that post in fifty-three years.*

I was a doctor present on Bloody Sunday. I treated the first two people wounded, and I pronounced four people dead in Glenfada Park. In the circumstances, the fact that the Widgery Tribunal didn't want my evidence is extremely suspicious.

I was standing at the corner of Rossville Street and William Street with Danny and Mickey McGuinness — two brothers-in-law of mine — and we were chatting. There was the familiar sound of rubber bullets, and CS gas going off. We were getting ready to move across to Free Derry Corner to listen to the speeches and go home. The riot was going on, but it was a normal Derry riot for that time.

Suddenly, I heard four shots which came from the back of the march in Upper William Street. I turned to Danny and said, 'That's different.' And within a couple of minutes some young boy came running down the street and asked me would I come because two people had been shot. I was amazed. So I went to Mrs Sheils' house where I must have spent about 20 minutes working with the Knights of Malta people, getting Damien Donaghey and John Johnston ready for the ambulance.

Then I was told that someone was shot dead outside, which I didn't believe. It was Gerard Donaghey. When I went out to see, Raymond Rogan had already taken him to hospital. I walked across Glenfada Park and I saw another man lying on the steps with two or three young fellows doing first aid. I opened his coat to see if I could get a heartbeat; there was a lot of blood and I realised he was dead. But I didn't say anything to the first-aiders. I said, 'Keep on working, and we'll get an ambulance as quick as we can.' I didn't want them to panic. I thought it was better if they were occupied.

Just after that, I met Leo Day who was in charge of the Knights of Malta. I said, 'Leo, look, this situation's pretty bad. Will you try and get on a telephone and call some ambulances as quick as possible?' I'd been told that there were some other people dead in a house in Abbey Park. So I went across into the Carrs' house where Jim Wray and Michael Kelly were lying dead. Someone told me to go next door, and that's where I found William McKinney. So there were four dead and two wounded, and I says to myself, my God, what's going on here, are they going to shoot us all?

I stayed with William McKinney until he died. He was quite calm, and died very well, and I hope that I would die as well he did. He said to me, 'I'm going to die, doctor,' and I said, 'Well I hope not. If we can get an ambulance and get you to hospital, you may be OK'. I thought it wasn't fair to say anything else to him. When I saw the internal injuries he had at the post-mortem, I didn't think he would have survived. There was no panic, no emotions, he just gradually slipped into unconsciousness, his pulse started to weaken and stopped. He died very peacefully and without pain, which I was very pleased about, because I didn't have my bag with me that day. I had been so convinced that there would not be any trouble. Shortly after William had died, the ambulances arrived. By this time I think I was in shock myself. We put the bodies into the ambulances, then we stood around smoking. The memory of it is the terrible silence of the place. I remember we talked in whispers.

The next morning I got a phone message from Cardinal Conway who asked me to represent him at the post-mortems, to take notes. I was present for eleven cases and didn't get home until twelve o'clock that night. I didn't see copies of the official post-mortems until 1997. I was absolutely amazed to find there were differences between my notes and the official reports because I thought we had all agreed, at the time, on what was recorded.

In the case of Barney McGuigan, for example, I had noted at the post-mortems a skull x-ray with approximately forty small pieces of metallic subject. I was horrified to find that there was no mention of any x-ray in the official post-mortem. The Saville Inquiry has now apparently found the x-ray and has pointed out that there is no doubt that these were bullet fragments which should have been removed at the time. The State Pathologist is the person who will have to answer that question.

When I made my submission to the Saville Inquiry, I mentioned five contentious cases: Barney McGuigan, Hugh Gilmour, Jim Wray, Kevin McElhinney and William McKinney. Those are the five that I think need particular investigation. In all of these cases full facts of the forensic pathology will have to be allied with eyewitness accounts so we can arrive at the truth. In fact, in the interim report for the Saville Inquiry, it is stated very clearly that in these five cases there were errors. Professor Simpson (now dead), who attended the Widgery Tribunal as an expert witness, agreed with the findings of the State Pathologist and the Assistant State Pathologist. He would have been the number-one person in London on forensic pathology at the time. Saville is calling the three pathologists who actually performed the post-mortems: Doctors Marshall, Carson and Press. It's fortunate that they're still alive after all this time.

There is also the case of Hugh Gilmour. It's recorded in my post-mortem notes that he had been shot twice: through his left arm and then through the chest. Two witnesses were called to the Widgery Tribunal, and Widgery accepted the evidence of one [of these people] and maintained that Hugh Gilmour had only been shot once. If Widgery had paid due attention to both eyewitness accounts, the story could have been put together accurately. I think that Hugh Gilmour was standing on the barricade shouting at the soldiers when he was shot through his left arm. Naturally, he turned and ran for safety, and as he turned around through 180 degrees, he was shot through the chest from right to left. That supports Geraldine Richmond's evidence which Lord Widgery ridiculed. At the time, there were no x-rays taken which would have proven conclusively whether or not he was shot twice but the forensic pathology evidence that we do have supports the statements made by both eyewitnesses.

Apart from those five cases, there is a certain amount of mystery around the deaths of young McDaid, Nash and Young. They were at the rubble barricade in Rossville Street about 250 yards from the walls — only a minor distance for an expert shot. They all died from a single bullet each which is consistent with sniper fire. And the passage through the body was identical in all three. The angulation from the walls to where they were was approximately 9 degrees. The trajectory of the bullet through the body was 45 degrees. But you can imagine, if there was a lot of gunfire going on, they wouldn't be standing straight up, they'd be slightly stooped, which would increase that angle, and that's what I think happened. Saville's interim report said that it wouldn't be possible to draw any clear conclusions about their deaths from the forensic evidence, and that the real story would have to rely on proper eyewitness accounts. At least they accepted the point, whereas Widgery didn't even entertain it.

And why were they placed in a Saracen and not taken to hospital by ambulance like all the other dead and wounded? I remember Fr Mulvey coming into the house in Abbey Park where I was attending William McKinney. He was angry as he told me about three people who had been thrown into the Saracen like pieces of meat. At the time I couldn't really take it in, it was so shocking. And then I found out that other people were killed.

What is striking too is the number of people who were shot in the back or the side whilst running away. It's also important that certain people were wounded first and shot dead afterwards: Jim Wray, Hugh Gilmour and possibly William McKinney. Some of the witness accounts say that he went to help Gerry McKinney, even though he was already shot himself. And [in all] only two bullets were recovered from the dead. Why?

Watching the Saville Inquiry from the public gallery, I have felt on many occasions that the unfortunate witness up in that lonely box is there defending their own integrity and their own life. You'd think they were on trial for a murder charge. They weren't responsible for the murder, but that's the way they're treated, and it's regrettable.

The Inquiry should also look at the whole question of post-traumatic stress disorder in witnesses. One witness — a first-aider from the Knights of Malta — was trying to describe what had happened to her, but she had a loss of memory, which is quite acceptable in a case of post-traumatic stress, and the counsel for the army said to her 'What were you doing in this time you had lost your memory?'

When Don Mullan's book came out, around the twenty-fifth anniversary, it was the first time a large number of people in this town started talking about the events, and where they were and what happened. And [then] we're asked to go along and give evidence at a legal inquiry. One witness was asked about the exact trajectory of a bullet fired above his head. I don't think any of us ever realised that we were going to be tied down to this sort of detail in giving evidence. If a good barrister has a bad case, what he's paid to do is put as much snow on the facts as he can, and discredit the witness. People are frightened of giving evidence, because there's a very clear attempt to belittle them.

On the positive side, [there are] at least fifty witnesses giving evidence about the shooting from the walls. That was never even considered by Widgery. Also, for the first time ever, people are being given the chance to state what they saw, what they heard and felt, which they weren't asked to do at Widgery because very few eyewitnesses were called. The weight of evidence tells its own story.

Bloody Sunday has stayed with me. I was very scared on the Sunday, but my personal anniversary is the day afterwards. Going through all those post-mortems was an awful ordeal.

EILEEN DOHERTY-GREEN & TONY DOHERTY

Eileen Doherty-Green was widowed on Bloody Sunday when Paddy Doherty was shot. He was a steward on the march that day and worked as a plumber's mate at the DuPont factory. Paddy was shot as he tried to crawl to safety in the forecourt of the Rossville Flats. He bled to death there because no one could get to him to help, as the Paras' firing was so heavy. Another man, Bernard McGuigan, tried to reach him but was killed instantly.

Tony was 9 years old when his father died. He was a spokesperson for the Bloody Sunday Justice Campaign. Tony is now the manager of a cultural and educational centre in the Bogside–Brandywell area of Derry.

EILEEN DOHERTY-GREEN

It must have been about quarter-to-five. Somebody had told me that my son, Patrick, was in the Bogside ... when I heard that, I went straight home to see if he was there because, at this stage, I had realised that they were shooting live bullets. My first thought was to see that the child was safe. On the way home my husband's cousin stopped me to tell me that [Paddy] was shot. He didn't tell me he was dead, but I think he knew.

When I was walking up home, I stopped a friend I knew in a car and he offered me a lift over to Altnagelvin Hospital. A few people I knew were there. I met Fr O'Gara and a friend of my husband's. The priest thought that my husband was one of the injured — he fitted the description of one of them. But when he went up to enquire, it was somebody else, so the priest accompanied my husband's friend to the morgue and Paddy was the second body he looked at. I'm glad I didn't go into the morgue because I heard the sight of all the bodies was terrible.

So then I had to come home and tell the children that their father was dead. I didn't believe that something like that could happen. To be quite honest with you, it was just like a dream. It wasn't that I didn't believe it, but how could this happen? And as you can see from the photograph of him crawling along, he was clearly unarmed. I think it's a unique thing that most of the people who were killed were photographed alive on the day.

We left home together to go on the march and took a short-cut up to the Creggan through the cemetery. It was the first time we ever did that and that was the last walk I had with him — through the cemetery. He was a member of the Civil Rights Movement and a steward on the march. We said our cheerio and that was the last time I saw him alive. When he left me he had his hanky tied around his arm because the stewards that day wore a white hanky.

Paddy was 31 when he died and I was 29. We had been married eleven-and-a-half years; I missed him a lot. People would say to me, 'God you're left with an awful handling,' as they say in Derry. I didn't really know what they were talking about because although I had six children, they were well brought up. My husband would have had to call them [only] once and they would come. He was a very good father but he was ... disciplined. So I hadn't really got much to do, he had them reared more or less, the older ones anyway. They were very good. I couldn't say that they were ever any trouble — I was lucky. I just coped, that's all I can say. The eldest was 10½, and the youngest was seven months. I'm the oldest of thirteen, I had my mother and my father and my family around me for support.

We are not looking for an apology. You only apologise when you've done something wrong and, according to the British Government, they haven't. An apology, to me at this stage, would be an insult. I think we deserve more than that. In some people's eyes, our relatives are still gunmen or bombers. After thirty years, let the truth out and be fair to the families of the people that were killed and wounded ... let us get on with the rest of our lives.

TONY DOHERTY

I was playing marbles for about 20 minutes on the corner of the street. All of a sudden the fellow I was playing with, Gutsy McGonigle, says, 'Your father has been shot; I saw him getting carried into an ambulance in the Bogside.' I said, 'If you're telling me lies, I'll get you tomorrow.' But sure enough as it turned out....

A distant cousin turned up and started tidying up [the house]. She wouldn't answer when I followed her out to the kitchen and asked her if something was wrong. So I knew then that there was something bad on the horizon. But I kept it to myself, hoping against hope. It must have been eight o'clock, or half-eight, when my mother and a few of her sisters and brothers, my grandfather and grandmother came back. I had been sitting on the stairs. My mother says, 'Your father has been shot dead.' I knew for definite then.

I remember him as a very ordinary man who was trying to rear a family in very extraordinary circumstances. On a Friday, he would always come home from work with sweets and chocolate in his pocket. He had no time for soldiers or police. During the Battle of the Bogside, for instance, my father would have been away for three nights running. Everybody was needed to defend the area. There was a really impending sense of danger and invasion by the B Specials.

I remember seeing all the coffins and having this abiding sense of disaster and doom and sadness. I was completely overwhelmed by the occasion as a child, although I'm nearly sure I didn't cry at the funeral. In the last few years, I've tended to become more emotional about it than I had in the past.

During the wake, I went to buy bread or milk. When I walked into the shop, the woman turned around and whispered something to her husband. I remember her not taking any money and sending me back with the messages.

I was just turned 9 and had to grow up quickly. I remember missing my father very badly for a good number of years, maybe until I became a mid-teenager. Then the Bay City Rollers and stuff started taking up my time. Since I became a father I've started thinking about what I missed. I tend to think of the sadness of it all sometimes. I think my wife would have got on great with him. He was just out of his twenties really, with six children. Now, looking back, it was around the time of the wake that my life and a whole lot of other people's lives were destined to change forever. People see me as first and foremost the son of one of the Bloody Sunday victims, which I don't always welcome but I can understand.

The mid-1970s wasn't a very nice peaceful time for people to grow up in. You were virtually in the middle of a war zone, stuff happening all around you almost every day. If I look back on it now, the chances of somebody like me not joining the IRA at that stage were very slim. I'm sure it was as much a response to what was happening on the street as it was to trying to live with the legacy of Bloody Sunday. You could almost have pointed in that direction in 1972. I went to prison between 1981 and 1985, was released in April 1985. [I] went back to university, and I'm now involved in community development within the same area that I was brought up in. I don't have any regrets really.

I have to live with the fact that my father is gone thirty years. Now, the injustice around the issue is probably harder to take than the actual killing itself. It's as if the wake period has been prolonged.

The Inquiry raises enormous issues for people who are involved in its outcome. I feel the cost is worth it, personally speaking. Yet it is only a means to an end: establishing the truth and overturning the conclusions of the Widgery Report. The process itself of the Inquiry is important in that [there is] exposure of the British Army and the nature of their involvement in Ireland. Nobody knows that better than the British Army and the Ministry of Defence.

Comparisons are made between the Saville Inquiry and the South African Truth and Reconciliation Commission. The difference is that in South Africa the Commission was seen as a means towards reconciliation, whereas here, the representatives of the soldiers have tried to turn it into an inquisition of the people of Derry. They have also tried to criminalise witnesses. In that sense the opportunity for reconciliation has been damaged for the ordinary person.

Saville wouldn't like to be described as 'Widgery Mark II' — a byword for judicial injustice, not just here but also abroad. But the law is an imperfect vehicle for getting at the truth, particularly when dealing with national issues. It is not the best vehicle for dealing with historical injustice. When the time comes and we have the final report, people will have to deal in resolute terms with closing the issue as a running injustice.

KAY DUDDY

Jackie Duddy was 17 years old when he died in the courtyard of the Rossville Flats. The first to die on Bloody Sunday, he came from a family of fifteen children and was a promising young boxer. He was shot through the left arm and the bullet came out through his chest. Kay Duddy was nearly 26 years old when her brother was killed; she had been helping to look after the family since the death of their mother.

At the time, we didn't have a phone in the house so I went over to the local community centre to phone the hospital. I don't know to this day whether it was a nurse or who it was answered the phone. I said, 'I'm Jackie Duddy's sister. I've reason to believe he was hurt down the town this afternoon.' A few minutes had elapsed when she came back and said, 'Jackie Duddy was dead on admission.' I just remember screaming and crying and throwing the phone up in the air. Then I had to go back and waken my daddy, who was asleep from his night shift, and tell him. Well, as you can imagine, he was upset — he nearly went crazy.

At the funeral it poured down with rain, it never ceased. I just remember hordes of people. They wanted to show their solidarity. We had to squeeze into the chapel. I think I have locked the actual events away in the back of my mind. There's an aunt of mine who maintains that I wasn't at the funeral because I had collapsed on the steps of the chapel and had to be taken home. I don' t remember. So … as I say, it was just … I don't know, it was just like a nightmare. For years afterwards I didn't want to talk about it, how Jackie had been shot down like a dog in the street. It didn't make any sense.

He was wee, quiet, insignificant, very hard to rile. My mammy, God rest her, had this wee rocking chair because she was a great fan of Val Doonican. It was a great novelty when it came into the house — you can imagine fifteen people plying to get into it. Jackie used to come home at lunch-time and as soon as he had his lunch, he'd get straight in the rocking chair and doze off for about 10 minutes before he went back to his work. And we used

to step on his toes and all that, to try and aggravate him in the way families do. But it took an awful lot to get him into a bad temper. His ambition was to box in the Olympics for Ireland; it was the love of his life. He really had no political affiliation. You never forget that smile on his face, he was so proud when he brought his trophies home.

People think you wouldn't miss one out a family of fifteen, but I think the more you have in a family, the more you miss a person. A big hole was left. Whenever there were weddings and stuff, he was always missing. Christmas, all you could do was buy him flowers: wreaths for the cemetery. He would have been 47 this year.

In the immediate aftermath of Bloody Sunday, the house raids started. They had murdered our brother and then they were coming in and dragging us out of our beds at five and six o'clock in the morning, herding us into one room like sheep and asking us our names and ages.

I mean, they could have told you what you had for your breakfast. It was so farcical, but it was frightening. I think they did it to try and make themselves feel better — make us feel like the criminals, instead of [us having] being sinned against. This went on for five years. I had five brothers left and they were often told, 'Oh, we got one of you, it will not be long 'til we get the rest of you.' I don't understand why all my brothers didn't join the IRA. We're so lucky that they didn't take that road because they were being persecuted into it.

We weren't allowed to discuss Jackie's death in the house at all. I think my Daddy's fear might have been the more we talked about it, the more angry we would have got. I remember a few years after it him saying, 'Don't

ever go out looking for revenge, because these boys have to live with themselves. Their consciences will get the better of them.' I don't feel bitterness towards the men who actually pulled the trigger, but I do feel that the truth has to be told. It was buried along with Jackie and the others.

I had a Protestant minister staying with me in January 1997, the Rev. Terence McCaughey, from Dublin. He should have come and spoken at the original march in 1972, [but] he couldn't make it as his wife had taken ill. So he was here on the twenty-fifth anniversary and helped me to go on my first march. He says, 'Kay, I'll help you to take your first step forward.' Before that, I couldn't bring myself to go. I just had this fear that Bloody Sunday was going to happen again.

With this new Inquiry, people are getting a chance to tell their stories. They were denied that opportunity at the Widgery farce, as I call it — I wouldn't call it an inquiry. Widgery only added insult to injury, slandering the dead and making them out to be nail-bombers and gunmen. It's equally important for the soldiers to get a chance to tell their stories too. I don't see how they can say they're under any security threat after thirty years. Nothing happened at the Widgery Tribunal, and if anything, it surely would have happened then. As regards the outcome of the Inquiry itself, I would say cautiously that I'm optimistic. If I wasn't, I wouldn't be there. I have been every day if at all possible, and it's wearing me down, I must say.

Our support group, Cúnamh, is so important right now. Not just for the families and the wounded, but for the public — the people of Derry — because they need somebody there to pick up the pieces. I met one fellow coming out after he had given his evidence. I thanked him, because I think people are very brave coming forward. He cried on my shoulder, saying he felt he'd been a coward for twenty-nine years. I said, 'You have to realise you were running for your life.' How many people out there have not forgiven themselves for running away? Survivor guilt — a big thing in this town, without a doubt.

My dearest wish is that the truth be told so that we can finally lay them to rest with a wee bit of peace and dignity. I feel sad that so many lives were lost as a result.

JOE FRIEL

Joe Friel was 20 years old on Bloody Sunday. He was shot in the chest as he ran for his life, but survived his injury. He worked at the local tax office and retired from the Inland Revenue twenty-three years later on grounds of ill-health — he was suffering from panic attacks and stress. He didn't speak publicly about his experience on Bloody Sunday until 1998.

I was the oldest of seven children. My grandad was a soldier. My great-uncles were soldiers in the First World War. My father was a soldier in the Second World War and worked for the Army right up until he retired. [He was also] in the Territorial Army. I was taken to their Christmas do's at the barracks when I was a kid. So, it just shows you, anybody could have been shot. I hadn't a political thought in my head. Though it was an anti-internment march, I went on it for the *craic* — round that time a march was a great place to meet people.

When the rioting started, after it hit William Street, I left the march. Both my brother and I had been on it but we never met as it was so big. I decided to go home to the Rossville Flats where I lived, to get a cup of tea and then go on to the meeting at Free Derry Corner. That's when I heard the first series of bangs; I thought it was rubber bullets. Hundreds of people started to run past me down Chamberlain Street, so I ran too. I was trying to get into the Rossville Flats along with everyone else. Imagine two to three hundred people trying to get up one flight of stairs. I was jostled out onto Rossville Street. Well, it was no place to be. I heard the shooting. So I made a run over to Glenfada Park. And as I ran, I could see one or two people falling, but luckily didn't realise the significance. I probably saw them getting shot but it didn't compute. It was just panic, looking to get out of there. I was nearly out of Glenfada Park when a wee boy, Gregory Wild, shouted, 'There's the Brits!' I instinctively turned round and saw three Paras. The one in front was shooting from the hip. As I heard 'bang, bang, bang', I felt just a light tap and the blood started to gush out of my mouth. I started shouting,

'I'm shot! I'm shot!' I fell against a wooden fence, staggered round the corner, fell down, and as I did, there were three fellows who lifted me.

They carried me into a house across in Lisfannon Park where a Knights of Malta girl, Evelyn Lafferty, gave me first aid. A lot of old dolls appeared out of nowhere — I presume they had run into the house. They were saying the Rosary around me, so I thought it was lights out. I was continuing to gush blood. Then some fellows decided to take me over to hospital in a car. We were on the way over when the Army stopped us and they were manhandled out of the car and taken away. A soldier got into the car and turned around and said, 'You shouldn't have been playing with guns.' I kicked the seat. He said, 'Well, if that's your attitude, we're staying here. You can die, you Irish bastard.' Shortly afterwards, a policeman got into the car and they drove me to the Army post under the bridge. A fellow came and put a big yellow bandage on my chest. After some time, I was taken to the hospital in an Army ambulance along with Paddy Campbell who had been shot too. The soldier later tried to frame me, saying that I had confessed I had been carrying a gun.

When I finally got to the hospital, Fr O'Gara gave me the last rites. Later on, before the operation, Fr Rafferty gave me the last rites again. Bad enough getting it once, but twice....

I couldn't actually see the wound because of where I was shot, high up on my chest. Probably the shock would have killed me. All I knew was just throwing up blood ... blood galore. The day seemed to drag. A minute seemed like an hour — the thought of dying makes you hold onto

every minute. They gave me a jab under the arm to put me to sleep. I still remember to this day they had to give me a second one such was my will not to be knocked out. I thought I would never wake up again.

It was several hours before my family got word. I was the last one they thought would be shot. I was quiet, shy, reserved. It completely changed my personality. I would say — funny enough — it turned me into a sort of extrovert to cover it up. Before Bloody Sunday, I didn't smoke or drink, I was a pioneer.

As the years went on, I bottled it all up. My wife will tell you, it was a taboo subject. At the time, counselling was unheard of. The only time I ever talked about it was when I was out, I'd had a few jars and maybe it was sometime round the anniversary. You would always get the person who would come over and say, 'What was it like to get shot?' I would just give them the briefest of details. My own son didn't know about it until he was 10 or 11 years old. I started taking panic attacks around 1989 and the doctor recommended I go to a psychotherapist. I was there for about a year, once a week. She coaxed it out, bit by bit. And the more I talked about it, [it] helped. I owe her a big debt.

It always affects me that Jim Wray, a fellow I knew, was shot right behind me — presumably in the same lot of shots. I stayed on my feet and got round the corner but Jim fell to the ground. The soldier came over and put a bullet in him as he was lying there. So that's my nightmare. If I had fallen to the ground shot too, it was lights out. But somehow the momentum kept me going.

You're talking in terms of split seconds. I turned around and that's what saved me. Otherwise I'd have been shot through the back. The bullet went the whole way along my chest but was deflected by the bone. I'd go on holiday and wear a tee-shirt, I was always conscious of the scar. Harry Bennett, the surgeon, said, 'A few inches either way, you were dead, it could have been straight through the back and through the heart.' I remember them taking my photograph at the hospital because my particular wound was so uncommon. The doctor told me that only eight soldiers in the British Army survived it in the last world war.

For years, I've been classed as a gunman by Widgery even though I wasn't wearing my glasses that day. If I was a sniper or a gunman, what was I doing with no glasses on? Another point that has never been made [is that] of all the injured that went to the hospital, not one was forensically tested. If we were gunmen or bombers, where's the forensics? There wasn't a swab taken off anybody.

I would like to think that the soldiers who did the shooting, as well as the higher-ups who sanctioned it and covered it up, would have some qualms of conscience. But look at Colonel Wilford. How do you forgive somebody that shows no remorse? I can forgive the Company Sergeant-Major who went on TV around the twentieth anniversary and apologised for that day. That man has had the courage to come forward. Where's the rest? I would like to actually get a name and see the face of the person who had tried to take my life. I could give him maybe a bad look and walk away and say, 'Why let so insignificant a person ruin my life?'

PROFESSOR TERENCE O'KEEFFE

Terence O'Keeffe was 31 years old on Bloody Sunday. At the time, he was a Roman Catholic priest and a lecturer in philosophy at the New University of Ulster in Coleraine. After his ordination in 1966, he had gone to study in Paris where he witnessed the student revolution of 1968. He was interested in radical theology and was also involved in an association of Irish priests, which took trade unionism as its inspiration.

After the march, the crowds were milling around Free Derry Corner and the announcement came that the rally proper was to start with an address from Fenner Brockway. Down at William Street, there was a certain amount of stone-throwing which was standard Derry-youth–Army confrontation. I was among a number of staff and students who had gone from the University at Coleraine to protest against internment. I wanted to make sure that none of the students were caught up in the stone-throwing, and that's why I found myself in the lower end of Rossville Street with another priest, Denis Bradley.

We were at the corner of Glenfada Park beside a gable wall, close to the rubble barricade, looking down towards William Street, in a small crowd of perhaps about twenty or thirty people. The loudspeaker was on and someone had begun to address the meeting down at Free Derry Corner, when we heard the revving of engines. Three army vehicles came up Rossville Street very fast and purposefully. My memory is of groups of soldiers descending and dispersing; I have no idea how many. Some took a kneeling firing position. The picture was somewhat hazy, because of the [CS] gas.

Some young fellows were standing in various little groups on the rubble barricade, a few yards away, throwing stones at the soldiers without very much effect. The soldiers began firing. Then I saw one of the lads close to the barricade go down, holding his stomach. He wasn't moving and, in my naïvety, I assumed that he had been hit in the stomach with a rubber bullet. Four others went out and carried him in. It was only when we turned him over [and] we saw the exit wound that we knew he was dead. Denis Bradley gave him the last rites.

When we next looked across there were three young fellows lying at the rubble barricade. They seemed to be dead. At that stage, an older man came running out and he went down. He lay there for some time with his hand in the air. Denis wanted to go out to them, but we decided it was too risky. There was fairly constant firing. So he gave them absolution at a distance.

My attention was caught by another young fellow [Kevin McElhinney] who was trying to crawl to the entrance of the Rossville Flats, across the street. People in the doorway were shouting, urging him on. Just as he reached the doorway he was shot. At this stage, we were all very frightened. Denis and I were trying to stop people panicking. Four young lads wanted to make a run for it across the car park of Glenfada Park. We were trying to hold them back but three of them ran out from the gable wall and were picked off. It became clear that there was nothing to do but just wait. It seemed like a long time, because all Denis and I could try to do was keep people calm, particularly when we saw the three young fellows killed as they tried to run away.

Not long after that, we were arrested. A soldier appeared from Glenfada Park; he was very aggressive and, at that point, I really thought I would be shot — that anything could happen. Within a short time, he was joined by other Paratroopers who came round both sides of the gable end and lined everybody up. Denis was allowed to go, I think because he was wearing his collar. I was not wearing mine and so I was put up against the wall. My

memory is of being hit several times. I said I was a priest and asked to attend to the wounded. The response was violence. All the soldiers seemed very pumped up and kept shouting and hitting us. Then we were marched down towards Kells Walk and loaded into an army lorry. I remember trying to protect my head from batons and rifles.

There were twenty-nine of us. I remember that it was a very frightening experience. There was a middle-aged woman who kept abusing the Paratroopers. She was really going for them, calling them 'murderers' and 'scum'. Unfortunately, as they got enraged, they didn't hit her, they hit me and others on the back and head. So I kept praying for this woman to shut up. We were driven to Fort George and literally kicked out of the lorry. It is the only time I've ever seen or participated in a gauntlet. When the tailgate was dropped, there were two lines of seven or eight Paras on each side with batons, hose pipes and rifles. We were invited to run for it. I took quite a few blows and was glad of the heavy coat I was wearing.

We were held in a very cold room and ordered to stand and grip barbed wire. Then each person was interviewed by what I presume to be RUC Special Branch, because certainly the assumption being made was that the scoop operation had picked up key IRA personnel. I was asked my name — my second name happens to be Mícheál, the Irish form. So I said, 'Terence Mícheál'. He looked up and he said, 'We're not speaking fucking Irish here, we're speaking English.' So I said, 'Well, fine, but my name

on my passport is Mícheál.' So he wrote, 'Michael'. And he said, 'What do you do for a living?' When I told him, he looked up, crossed 'Michael' off, and wrote 'Mícheál'.

Then I was taken to another room to await charging. At this stage the Paratroopers returned to the holding room. There was a fair amount of idle brutality. I remember particularly one very scary soldier and another Paratrooper, who was called 'F'.* They were guarding us and took great delight in standing on young fellows' feet and then kneeing them very hard in the groin. They would wander in and suddenly hit somebody. The place was extremely cold and some heaters on stands were brought in. The two Paras forced two young kids to put their faces right up against the heaters and stand in a strained position for a long time. If they tried to move away, they were battered. One of them was asked if he wanted a drink. He said yes and was told to open his mouth. Then 'F' spat into his mouth.

Afterwards, I wrote an official letter of complaint to General Tuzo. I still have a copy — allow me to quote briefly:

Both Fr Bradley and myself were refused permission, on at least three occasions, with a good deal of verbal abuse, foul language and some physical assault, to go to the assistance of the wounded and dying…. Your soldiers seemed unconcerned … and used unnecessary abuse and violence towards us to make that point. I witnessed conduct that was

---

* The soldiers cannot be named and have therefore been allocated letters and numbers, for identification purposes, by the Saville Inquiry.

sickeningly brutal and a disgrace to any uniform. Assaults were committed in a sadistic manner on a number of people, particularly youths aged from about fifteen to nineteen years....Your soldiers sir, were in obviously good form ... without exception smiling in obviously sadistic enjoyment of their actions.

Eventually I was charged. 'F' came up to me and said, 'You were throwing stones.' I said, 'I'm a Roman Catholic priest and a lecturer in philosophy and I don't throw stones.' He kicked me very hard in the groin and said, 'You should have been wearing your fucking dog collar then.' I was released about 11.40 p.m., after about 7 hours.

Afterwards, an amnesty was later granted to those arrested for stone-throwing and rioting, and I was told that no action would be taken against the soldiers.

I got over my injuries. The horror of seeing people killed haunted me for a long while. I'd certainly waken up sweating, so I must have had nightmares. My time in Paris in 1968 had been exhilarating and sometimes frightening, but Derry was simply horrendous.

JOHN DUDDY

John Johnston was John Duddy's brother-in-law. He was shot on Bloody Sunday and died of his wounds five months afterwards. He was 59 years old and the oldest person to die as a result of the shooting. He was one of the first to be shot, some 15–20 minutes before the rest of the shooting began. John Duddy was 49 years old at the time.

John Johnston was married to my sister. He was a businessman; he used to be dressed in a Crombie coat — pretty distinguished looking, a big fellow. He was going down to see to a wee man who had moved recently, in case he'd be nervous with the demonstration going on.

To my mind, he was sacrificed that day, him and young Bubbles [Damien] Donaghey. The way I figured it, they were shot 15 minutes before anyone else, to draw fire if there was anyone there. There wasn't, you know.

When the march set off from the Creggan, I said to a couple of the other fellows who were walking down, 'I've a feeling something bad is going to happen today.' I thought the Army would wade in and knock the hell out of anybody they caught. I didn't think, then, that they would be firing live rounds. When we got down to the Bogside, I left the march to go down to the barricade in William Street. I felt pretty badly about the march being stopped — we only had to go another 50 yards into the Guildhall Square. The water cannons started and I got sprayed with blue dye, so I decided to come away. Next thing, the first Saracen came flying, turned and stopped. You could count — just 1, 2, 3 — and all the doors burst open at the one time. Paras came out and started firing. We sheltered behind Kells Walk ... they must have bypassed us. They headed up Rossville Street towards Free Derry Corner. On my way home, someone called out to me, saying that my brother-in-law had been shot. I made my way up to Creggan. I had to get washed, changed, get into the car and call to my sister, Johnnie's wife. I didn't say the state he was in, I just said, 'Look, I'm going to the hospital, Johnnie got injured.'

I had my son with me and my son-in-law — we were coming down in the car. When we got down as far as the Cathedral gates, Paratroopers stopped us. There were people already lined up against the chapel railings. I said, 'I'm on my way over to the hospital to see the brother-in-law that you bastards shot'. Aye, I was angry, very angry. They hauled us out of the car. I was put standing against the rails. I could see Fr Mulvey who was inside the grounds. One of the Paras said to me, 'Only there's so many around, you're a dead man.' Another boy, a Scotch man, said, 'Cool it, Gus.' They searched everyone. This went on for a while, then the order came for them to pull out and I heard the man in charge saying, 'Murder?' into the radio, and then laughing mockingly. I went to the back of the Saracen and I said, 'Have you the keys of the car?' The Paras said, 'Look in the boot.' As I turned, I was hit in the back — they threw my keys at me.

When I eventually saw Johnny, he had about four wounds on him, he had the leg of the trousers cut off, the sleeve cut off his shirt. The hospital was unbelievable — it was like a casualty station, they were all over the place. Johnny was calm which surprised me because he was the type of man that if he had cut his finger in the house, he would have been panicking. It could have been the shock at that time.

After I saw Johnny, I went around to see Joe Friel who was also in hospital. I went to his house on the way home to get word to his family. I remember that Joe was upset about the three fellows who were taking him to hospital in the car. They were pulled out and given a rough time.

Johnny didn't die for five months. It was after he got home that he started to get very vague. He was acting very strangely. The fall he took when he was shot gave him a brain tumour and he never recovered.

The Paratroopers were trained very intensively and that day was a chance to apply it. They were all geared up; this was their chance to shoot live targets — a lot of people that didn't count as far as they were concerned. Their idea was to teach them a lesson but it backfired. Apparently, afterwards, when they went back to barracks, they were boasting they had killed. The whole operation was callous.

Now, with this inquiry, they are clutching at straws trying to defend themselves.

MICHAEL McKINNEY

Michael's brother, William, was 27 years old when he was shot in the back by Paratroopers on Bloody Sunday. The eldest of ten children, he worked as a compositor on the local newspaper, The Derry Journal. *His passion in life was photography and Super 8 films. Michael was 20 years old at the time. He was the chairperson of the Bloody Sunday Justice Campaign and is now a family liaison worker at the Bloody Sunday Centre in Derry.*

I was on the march; everybody in my family was on it. Willie, as usual, would have been out with his cine camera. When the shooting started, I sought refuge in my aunt's house. Everything just went haywire. Her house filled up; it was a mass of people running in, screaming and roaring. Within a very short space of time there were reports coming in [that] there were five and six dead down at the barricade on Rossville Street. Later, I went to Mass and I remember Fr Rooney speaking about the terrible events. I didn't know about Willie.

Willie was a very mild, quiet person. My younger brother Joe, myself and Willie, we were all going steady at the time. At the weekends, if we were away at a dance, we would have waited on the others coming in. We might have made soup and sat and had a bit of *craic*. Willie would have been telling us stories about the people at *The Derry Journal* where he worked. He was good fun. At the time, Joe and myself would have had a sort of militant attitude and Willie would have been maybe more middle-of-the-road. There was many a late-night discussion. He was older than the two of us.

Willie died in Glenfada Park. He was photographed standing beside Michael Kelly who had been shot. He had probably seen a number of people being killed. I think he took a chance when he ran across the car park — stupidity or bravery, I don't know. Maybe instinct — he wanted to get away and was shot along with Joe Mahon.

Bloody Sunday was premeditated. Widgery, in his report, side-tracked on the truth a lot of times; but he did tell the truth on *one* occasion, when he said the soldiers weren't out of control. The whole thing was planned.

Derry was one place that bothered the Northern Ireland Government because of the no-go area. The Bogside, from 9 August 1971 until Motorman the following July, was the only place where they hadn't any control.

After Mass that evening, I went home to let my mother know I was OK. I remember seeing Fr McLaughlin's car parked close by and thinking there must be something wrong with one of my neighbours. I went in and our house was crowded with people; my mother was sitting, crying. My father came to me and he said, 'Willie is dead.' I broke down.

I remember, the following morning, my father wakened me with his crying. George, who would have been the next eldest to Willie, was sitting with him, saying, you have still five sons, trying to console him. And my father crying his eyes out saying why couldn't they wound him instead of killing him. It broke his heart.

I found out a few years ago, although at times I often wondered, that my mother grieved in private — she wouldn't grieve in front of us. She only told me then that she had been afraid of driving us into the IRA, and that was the reason. That was her fear — one death being enough. So it has taken its toll.

I thought I had accepted Bloody Sunday and the injustice of it, but then the Birmingham Six got out and, happy as I was for them, it pressed a button and I was full of anger. My first reaction was, what about the people that were killed on Bloody Sunday?

The only people that were ever going to do anything about Bloody Sunday were the families — we had to take it on. I was involved in the campaign from when it started

in 1992. It took five years to get the Irish Government on our side. For the first time in twenty-five years, the issue reached a new prominence. Along with that support and the uncovering of new evidence, the British were forced to set up a new inquiry.

Our concern at the minute is to have all the people who were killed and maimed on Bloody Sunday declared totally innocent. We'll wait until the Inquiry is over, to find out what Saville concludes — will he declare them all innocent? Then we'll see what we've got and take it from there.

Why should anybody who committed murder be above the law? Some might think the Army have immunity from prosecutions. Well my answer to that is that, ten years ago, people told us we were mad, that we'd never get anywhere taking on the British Government looking for an inquiry. Now we've done that. No matter what they throw in our way, no matter what obstacles, I'm here until the end.

MARY DONAGHEY

> *Gerard Donaghey was 17 years old in 1972 and worked at a local brewery. A thin lad, he was quiet and tidy at home. His sister, Mary, who was 24 years old, had brought him up for seven years. Her cousin, Damien 'Bubbles' Donaghey was shot in the leg that day. After his death, Gerard Donaghey was photographed by the Army with nail-bombs sticking out of his pockets. He had injuries to the abdomen, and new evidence shows that at least one of the nail-bombs would have exploded if he had had any on him when he was shot.*

[Mary has just had her photograph taken in Glenfada Park.]

That there's the first time I've ever been at the wall where Gerard was killed. In all those years, I never went across that way. I wasn't too sure where he was shot and I had to get his friend, Denis, to draw me a diagram. I've only the one brother now, I have no sisters. There was just the three of us. I was 24 at the time. Mammy and Daddy had died and I reared him from when he was 10, so he was a son as well as a brother. I would never go to bed until he would come in. Gerard was a very good young fellow. He was football-mad; there was never much bother with him really.

The doctor said if they could get him to hospital, there would be a chance of him living. So Raymond Rogan and Leo Young put him into the back seat of the car. But they were stopped by the Army and arrested. I always think about what was going through his mind, him dying on his own. They left him lying alone in the car until he drew his last breath. It makes me very angry. To think that he died in an Army post when they knew that they could have saved his life. That's when they planted the nail-bombs on him. He couldn't have got them into the trousers that he was wearing and the denim jacket was far too tight. Dr Kevin Swords, who saw him before he left for the hospital, didn't see the nail-bombs.

I was on the march and came home because I had my son — he was only a baby in a pram. I was sitting, knitting away, and happened to look out the window when I saw everybody running; [I] heard bangs. You would have hardly seen the people's feet hitting the ground, they were running that hard. So when I saw all Gerard's pals coming back, I said there's definitely something up. A young fellow came to the door and he says, 'Mary, your Gerard was shot dead today.' He just came straight out with it. If I had got hold of him, really, I would have thrown him over the railings. Then, Fr Rooney came and told me [Gerard] was dead. The army eventually released his body to the hospital around ten o'clock that night. We were back and forth to the hospital — every other body but Gerard's was there. My husband went to the morgue. 'They had no call even to lift the sheet,' he says. 'I knew him by the boots that he had on him.'

After Gerard's death, I started to go blind for spells. When I found it coming on, I used to put my son, Denis, in the playpen. I would sit until it would leave me. This lasted for five years. The doctor told me it was delayed shock. Sometimes, I would be setting the table, I would go to call him and then realise.... One night, I got this rare feeling there was somebody in the room with me. When I woke up, I could see him as plain as anything. Ach, God, I loved him so much. Well, he never really goes away. Perhaps it's because he was the youngest too. I find that it doesn't get any easier. Maybe it's because there was no justice done — they got away with what they did.

The new evidence coming out at the Saville Inquiry is overwhelming. I'm just waiting to see how it finishes. I find it hard. Away back during the campaign for the Inquiry, I was involved in organising things — now it's out of my hands. At the start, I didn't understand some of the words the lawyers were using. Also, I have my doubts

about the way the Army lawyers want to know about witnesses' backgrounds before 1972 instead of dealing with Bloody Sunday itself. I feel the community is being [put] out on trial. They are trying to undermine people and put them off coming forward. If I were to go out and kill someone, I would be hunted and brought up for it. I pray every night that their names be cleared. I wake up thinking about it.

Can the Army not come out and admit that they were wrong? I don't think it would hurt them. I know it may be in the past, but until justice has been done I cannot forgive anybody.

DANIEL McGOWAN & TERESA McGOWAN

Daniel McGowan was 37 years old on Bloody Sunday. He was shot in the leg as he tried to get away from the gunfire. At first, he did not believe it was actual shooting but sought cover along with other people anyway; then Hugh Gilmour collapsed at his feet. A short time later, Daniel came to the assistance of his friend, Paddy Campbell, who had been shot in the back. Afterwards, Daniel retired from his job as a maintenance man at DuPont and never worked again. At the time, he had been married to Teresa for eighteen years. She was expecting their ninth child. Afterwards, she worked nights as a supervisor in the Ben Sherman shirt factory, and also ran the home.

Daniel McGowan

I joined the march for the rally at Free Derry Corner as I wanted to hear Bernadette Devlin speaking. I had a couple of pals on the march from DuPont, I couldn't see them — it was a big crowd. I walked on down, got near Joseph Place. When I reached the telephone box, I heard firing. I said to myself, 'No, it's a backfire or something.' But everybody got down because shooting had started.

All of a sudden, a young fellow fell at the corner. He lived up in the flats. He had been running home and was hit as he was going in the door. It was a high-velocity bullet which hit him in the back and nearly blew him off his feet. A crowd of us gathered around and I said a prayer in his ear.

But the bullets started flying again, so I ran. I met a friend of mine, Paddy Campbell, an older man who worked in Derry Docks. He was staggering, he was shot in the back. I got hold of him; he was very heavy and he was wearing a big overcoat — and on a fine day like that! I helped him into an alleyway at the back of Joseph Place, and one of his nephews came running up, and a pal with him. They grabbed Paddy and said to me, 'Thanks, mister.'

The alleyway was jammed with people; you couldn't get in there. I said to myself, 'I'm not going to get shot in the open.' So I made me way up the steps at the back of the flats. Then I looked up, saw the green uniform of the Army and turned back. A bullet came flying and took a piece out of the wall above me, which hit my head. I would have got away, but it kind of stunned me. Then, the next bullet hit me in the leg and lifted me up in the air. I think they were shooting from the Derry Walls. Two young fellows came out; the bullets were still flying as they pulled me into the alleyway. I had to wait for a while until the shooting stopped and a car could be got to take me to hospital. But Billy Long and Jackie Morrison brought me up home instead. They decided it would be safer to get an ambulance to the house as the Army were stopping cars going over to the hospital.

Teresa McGowan

I remember being up at the upstairs window — me and the younger ones — watching the march, and the bands coming down the road. I thought to myself, 'Gosh, I'd love to be on that march,' but I had too many youngsters. I said, 'Ah well, it's not for me.' I had too much to do at the weekends to make up for my time out at work. But I think half of Derry was on that march. I was pregnant at the time and working nights in the factory; I worked up to the Friday night and the child was born on the Sunday. Two weeks after she was born, I was back at work again as I was concerned about the family income. Danny changed so much and I had to care for him and the kids. My mother lived next door and gave me and a good hand; this was how I could work. I had to manage; it was pride kept me going. It was hard but I got through it all. Hardness does you no harm, it makes you appreciate things.

That afternoon, when I saw Billy Long at the door, I thought he was looking for Danny. He beckoned me and when I looked into the car, I couldn't believe it was my

husband. He was very old-looking, lying there semi-conscious, and his whole complexion was grey. Billy Long explained, 'We're afraid to go over to Altnagelvin because they're arresting [people].' We carried Danny in and put him on the settee. His leg was all hanging down like broken sticks and he started crying with the pain. I could feel it was all smashed, I remember getting a pair of scissors and cutting the trouser leg to see. There was confusion — neighbours and all were coming in. His brother arrived, and then the ambulance. At that point Danny was panicky, talking very fast and loud. He was in hospital for 8 weeks. As the days went by, you'd hear the names of the other people who were shot.

Danny had always liked to work — [he] was never idle. He used to cut the children's hair and would organise to take them all away to a caravan during the holidays. He was a very dependable person. After he was shot, his nerves were bad. He was in the hospital with them for a while and he wasn't capable of work at all. Then he started to drink a lot more than ever, and being around the house really got him depressed. I think if Danny had taken a light job and gone back to work, he could have put it behind him. His hair went white and his health deteriorated; he got cancer about fifteen years afterwards. He took a tumour in the floor of his mouth, and by the time he got his operation, it had become a major thing. He was always a very fit man. Now he doesn't eat much — he chokes very easily, I don't know what keeps him going.

Everybody's marriage changes through the years, but I would say that it was Danny that changed after Bloody Sunday. He was very protective of the children. They weren't allowed to go anywhere, so they thought he was far too strict, but it was because of the Troubles. They would clear off the street when they saw him coming. I would say that Danny's personality is not what it was. We could sit here all day with the family here visiting and Danny will not have two words to say to them — there's not great conversation. As the children were growing up, they could have been great pals; that just didn't happen.

One night lately, my eldest son, who is now 41, was here. He said, 'You know, Daddy, you never asked me to help you, or do anything for you.'

The time he was compensated for his injury, he bought nothing for the house. He doesn't mix with anybody, doesn't know how life changes. It's that TV and him. I go to the Saville Inquiry; he doesn't. I like to sit down there at the Guildhall because you are learning something. There's lots of things coming out of the Inquiry now — it's like piecing together a jigsaw puzzle.

I was up in Buncrana recently. I looked at the couples enjoying themselves and thought, that should be Danny and [me]. We shouldn't be spending our older years like this.

RAYMOND ROGAN

In 1972, Raymond Rogan was chairman of the local Abbey Street and Area Residents' Organisation and was married with five children. He has had a life-long commitment to youth and community work, and now sits on statutory bodies for housing and health. Gerard Donaghey, who was 16 years old at the time, was carried into Raymond's house after he was shot.

It was a nice, sharp, cold, bright day, and spirits were very high. We were looking forward to making our point and had no idea what was in front of us.

It became clear the Army had blocked the lower part of William Street. Some young lads, not as tolerant as people of my age, began throwing stones. I went home [and] shortly afterwards, we saw people running past. We could hear shooting but thought it was plastic bullets. Then we became alarmed because it had a distinctively different sound. We looked out and saw people running; some came into our house to shelter and told us that the Army were shooting live rounds. Looking out my front window, I saw people leaning over somebody on the ground. I called one of them to bring him in and we laid him on the living-room floor. It struck me that he looked like a baby — he was very young. I don't know where the doctor, Dr Kevin Swords, came from — he examined him; he had a wound in his stomach.

My wife was anxious to find out who the lad was so we could let his people know. We couldn't find any identification on him at all. I patted his pockets: he was wearing very tight jeans, and a denim jacket. The doctor searched his pockets. A medal around his neck was the only thing we could find. If there had been nail-bombs on him, I wouldn't have let him be carried into my house because that would have been putting my family at risk.

My wife said a decade of the Rosary over him. The doctor suggested that he was in a bad way but if he could be got to hospital quickly, he would have a chance. I volunteered to take him, and he was carried out to my car, a white Cortina. He was put in the back across the knees of Leo Young who had helped carry him into the house. Leo had a brother shot dead that day, although he didn't know it at the time. As we set off, I could hear shooting but I kept going.

We were stopped in Barrack Street by soldiers from the Royal Anglians. I wasn't worried about being accused of anything wrong, only about getting straight to the hospital. I was really shocked at the attitude of the Army. They forcibly pulled us out of the car at gunpoint. [They] wouldn't let me explain that a doctor had advised [me to] get the young lad to hospital as quickly as possible. We were very roughly manhandled and told to stand facing the wall with our hands behind our heads. I could see my car sitting there, and nobody was making any attempt to do anything about the young lad who was still in the back.

I said, 'Look, that lad is going to die.' One of the soldiers lifted his gun, pointed it at me and said, 'Shut your mouth; one stiff is not enough for me' — something to that effect. For the first time, I actually feared for my life.

Shortly afterwards, I noticed the car had gone. After half an hour, we were taken in an armoured car to a temporary Army camp where we were body-searched with a sniffer device for traces of explosives. We were then transferred to the custody of the RUC. I asked to speak to the Superintendent of the police, Frank Lagan, or the Assistant Superintendent, who both knew me. Suddenly I heard an explosion. They said there were allegedly bombs in my car and they had blown the boot open. I was furious at that. My car was retained for forensic examination.

Later, I was released and told that the young man had died. It was 7.30 that evening when I came home and

learnt that so many [more] people had been killed. Nobody had expected it, and to be confronted with that kind of state violence was a great shock. I remember a terrible feeling of helplessness and anger, particularly because, despite our best efforts, Gerard Donaghey had been deliberately left to die in the back of my car.

Everything escalated after Bloody Sunday. The Bogside and Brandywell became a no-go area for the Army and the police. All the main routes in were barricaded. Life became very difficult for people, because things like bread and milk were not easily available. And if there were burst pipes or a fault in the electricity, none of these services could be maintained. This went on for about seven or eight months until Motorman. During that period, a local priest, Fr Denis Bradley, organised an election. We formed the Bogside Community Association — it was local self-government. I was elected to represent my immediate area and subsequently became its chairman for two years. We would meet with paramilitaries and the Army, the police and the statutory bodies — anybody who had an input into the situation — so it was quite a historical time.

Over the years, I did see quite a few horrific sights, but Bloody Sunday was the worst. I shudder to think what people felt like, walking past dead bodies, when they were arrested by the Paras. Widgery dismissed my evidence. They had photographs of Gerard Donaghey in the back of my car with nail-bombs in his pockets. I just could not believe it. There was definitely nothing in his pockets, absolutely nothing.

One can't help but think back to the Widgery Report and the conclusions he drew. Certainly the whole process of the new Inquiry is still iffy for a lot of people. It'll depend very much on Saville to recognise that there was an injustice, and have the will to declare that, and give his reasons.

The Ministry of Defence lawyers want access to Inquiry witnesses' personal files, from the intelligence point of view; I don't think it's relevant if they are giving evidence about what they experienced on Bloody Sunday. Also it's difficult for people not used to the legal process to comprehend why they are asked questions about minute and irrelevant details; it certainly upsets and confuses them.

If the MoD lawyers can sow confusion and get enough people to give incorrect evidence, the whole picture could change.

It's interesting, though, how some people are very single-minded in giving their evidence — it's very humorous at times with quick and very pertinent replies to the barristers.

I remember one person who comes from a Republican background, and he was asked, 'Do you know so-and-so, and what was he doing that day?' and he said, 'Oh, I'll let him answer for himself. I'm here to answer your questions, not to answer his!' But they're few and far between, people who have that kind of calmness.

JOHN KELLY

John Kelly is the eldest son in his family and was 23 years old when his brother was killed. He was the chairperson of the Bloody Sunday Justice Campaign and is now a family liaison worker at the Bloody Sunday Centre in Derry. John's brother, Michael, was 17 years old when he died and was the seventh of thirteen children. He attended college in Belfast where he was studying to become a sewing-machine mechanic. He came home every Friday night, went out dancing, and worked on Saturdays. He kept sixteen pigeons which his mother would let out for him during the week.

He fell just behind the rubble barricade across the street from the flats. I was standing outside Carr's house nearby, observing people attending to Gerry McKinney, when my brother-in-law, George Downey, called out to me. I ran over and helped put Michael in the ambulance. On the way to hospital, we counted thirteen of us, jammed in the front and out the back. Michael had no massive loss of blood. They put a Babygro* into the wound and bandaged everything tight. My mother was down in Rossville Street when the shooting began, in her sister's house. She saw Michael and called over to him to come in, and he disappeared. If he had heard her, it might have been a different story altogether.

He was dead on admission, but to be truthful, I think when I'd first seen him, he'd gone. My father came and did the formal identification in the morgue. At home, the house was packed. My mother was living in hope because someone had told her he had been shot in the ankle. But once we came in and said otherwise, that was it. That night was terrible. I blanked out a full day there was that much going on. I hardly remember the coffin coming home. Michael lay in the back bedroom and, although my mother was heavily sedated, around three or four o'clock in the morning, she dived into the room calling, 'Michael, son! Michael, son!' and lifted him bodily out of the coffin. We had to put him back in.

We had him until Wednesday. There wasn't a mark on his face and he was only 17. I always remember him lying in the coffin — it never leaves your mind. Before I was married, we shared the same bed and I used to wake up in the night with a warm back on me. Wee bits of memories like that…. He just wanted to learn his trade, go with his girl, look after his pigeons.

As my mother would say, the chain has been broken, because one of hers has gone. It nearly killed her. She still has his clothes — they are to be buried along with her. Like Mrs McDaid, when she died, her son Michael's clothes went with her. That shows you how Derry women think about their sons. We couldn't let my mother out of our sights; we followed her to Mass, we followed her down the town. But she doesn't remember anything for five years. There were occasions where she went missing and we would find her up in the cemetery. She would take a blanket up to put over the grave in the winter to keep him warm. Herself and Jim Wray's mother, they used to sit in the dark in the cemetery, the two of them chatting. I'd say Mrs Wray went to her death with a broken heart. My da died about eleven years ago — he took it bad. When he died, we found a big book — he had all the cuttings, all the newspaper clippings. So he handled it his own way.

It's been a long thirty years. I think it was expected of me, as the eldest son, to try and help. Everybody in the family pulled together. Otherwise my mother definitely would have died. Maybe that's one of the driving forces behind me in relation to this campaign. I want to see it come to a successful conclusion for my mother and all the families.

---

* An all-in-one baby's outfit.

My brother was classed as a nail-bomber and, according to the British, the Paras were on an arrest operation. But it's blatantly obvious that there was a plan to shoot people. They set out to destroy the Civil Rights Movement and to take the nationalists off the streets. But what they did was create hell for everyone — approximately 20 minutes' work cost the lives of hundreds of people in the Troubles.

Now the Army are not taking responsibility; they are on an IRA witch-hunt. They are trying to place IRA personnel on the march, saying that they shot at the British Army, who fired back in self-defence and killed our people. The Army are saying that, apart from the four-teen who died and those who were injured, there were thirty-four other victims, who were IRA men! Derry is a tight-knit community; to put it crudely, if somebody farts, everybody knows. Now, if somebody was shot dead on Bloody Sunday, that person's name would have been known; what about his family, his friends, his workmates?

Those Paras went in with intent to kill, so I believe that every one of them should be prosecuted, [and also] the people who planned it, and the people who gave the OK for it to happen — every one of them, right to the top. I'm talking about Edward Heath as well. My family and all the other families are entitled to justice — my brother is no different to any other person who is murdered. If we get to the truth of what happened that day, I believe there should be prosecutions. In January 1998, we were promised an open and transparent Inquiry; we've seen the Army trying to make it as difficult as possible for the Inquiry to get to the truth.

We lost the anonymity issue, which was ridiculous because we know the names of a lot of the soldiers, and we've seen their photographs. We've had the destruction of the weapons, including recently, the destruction of the weapons belonging to soldiers 'F' and 'G' — 'F' being the person who murdered Michael. So we are questioning the sincerity of the Minister of Defence and the Home Office.

It has been a long process and, at times, very difficult for families to sit and listen to witnesses describing the last moments of people's lives. Even the witnesses them-selves are under great stress — they sometimes collapse through reliving the emotion and trauma of seeing people being murdered before their very eyes. People talk about the pain of re-opening old wounds, but the wounds have never healed.

It's hard on the families and the injured to have to listen to the Army give their testimony. We have to face these guys and listen to their blatant lies. But we accepted the process of the Inquiry. It's ridiculous for people to say that the soldiers' lives are in danger, because we *want* those people here, we want to hear face-to-face why they murdered our people.

I've my life to live. I'll be 54 this year; over half my life has gone concerning the Bloody Sunday issue and I'll be glad to put it all behind me. It's hard dealing with it, living with this thing 24 hours a day, going to sleep and waking up in the morning thinking about it. I would like to think that if it were addressed truthfully and justly, it would ease the pain. Then I could move on.

MICHAEL BRIDGE

Michael Bridge was 25 years old in 1972. At the time, he worked as a coal carrier on the docks in Derry. He gave evidence at the Widgery Tribunal, but, like many other people, was very unhappy at the outcome. He did not speak again about his experience on Bloody Sunday until the announcement that a new inquiry was to be held. While acting as a steward on the march, Michael suffered CS gas inhalation and was hit by a rubber bullet before being shot in the leg.

I had been at the barricade in William Street where there was a bit of rioting. There were no more than a dozen of us trying to steward the crowd. We were trying to get them to go over towards Free Derry Corner and we were reasonably successful until the Army threw some CS gas and the rubber bullets. Then they used the water cannon and it broke up the crowd. The gas made most of the people around me sick, including myself. I threw up in a little lane nearby. I came back to William Street to see what was going on and was hit in the foot by a rubber bullet, so I sat down on the pavement.

The crowd started running and shouting that the soldiers were coming in. I cut down a lane and came out on waste ground where a Saracen was facing me directly. Soldiers jumped out and started firing live rounds. I turned on my heels to go back into Chamberlain Street. One of the soldiers fired over my head and hit the gable end of the first house in Chamberlain Street, opposite the bookies.

People coming down the street from the Rossville Flats were shouting about a young boy shot. I ran into the car park, saw him on the ground — he seemed to be dead. I turned towards the soldiers and I gave them a mouthful. It's a reaction I can't explain. Any rational person would have run away. I could sense bullets flying all around me; a fusillade of bullets spun me around and I was shot in the leg. It went straight through the upper thigh. I heard later that somebody saw me go down, he went straight to my house and told my father I was dead. He couldn't deal with it and took the dog out. But the family knew within half an hour that I wasn't dead.

Two men ran out and carried me into a house on Chamberlain Street. The front room was so crowded they laid me out in the back yard, where I was given a cup of tea and a cigarette. Two young boys from the Knights of Malta worked on my leg. Then Paratroopers came in and took everybody out of the house and lined them up against the wall. I remember, vividly, the people lined up outside getting stick from the soldiers — verbal abuse, pushing and hitting. I was carted out on a stretcher and put in an ambulance. I got one of the women to come with me in the ambulance to get her off-side. Everybody else in that house was arrested, including a man that helped me.

Sometimes, I'm just back in that house in Chamberlain Street again. The people who ran out to help that day, they were brave. I still know one of the men that helped me. If he hadn't done so, I would probably be one of the dead because at the time they were still firing.

It's unbelievable that a fully trained soldier could line you up in the sight of his rifle and shoot you when there was no danger to [him]. I was only 10 yards away and supposed to be throwing a nail-bomb at the time! I was lucky to be only shot in the leg.

At the hospital, I saw Joe Friel getting wheeled in after me. The blood was coming up his throat. I thought he was dying. I kicked at the door to get attention; eventually someone came in. Later, I was put in the same ward as Paddy Campbell, Alex Nash and Joe Friel. The four of us being together was a very big help. The reality of what happened only hit me when people came in to see us and when I saw the newspaper — I wasn't on the best of form. There was a mass of visitors: reporters, police, friends

and family. The ward never emptied — the hospital gave up trying to keep visiting hours. The day of the funerals was rough — we were on our own the four of us. To this present day, I never went to visit the graves.

The Inquiry should be proper, warts and all. Trying to follow it is, at times, difficult. It seems to be a situation of judge thyself; restrictions are being put on it by the very people who were responsible in the first place — the Ministry of Defence. They are doing it under the guise of protecting the soldiers' human rights. They have opened a can of worms and they are on a damage-limitation exercise.

It has given me sleepless nights. I don't see any reason why a person who was representing the British Government at the time can commit murder and maim people in the streets. If it had been the opposite way about and I had shot someone, I would have been held accountable.

GERALDINE RICHMOND

Geraldine Richmond was 18 years old at the time of Bloody Sunday, and was engaged to be married. The daughter of a mixed marriage, she worked as a cuffer in a shirt factory and enjoyed a lively social life, despite the Troubles. Like many people in Derry, Geraldine was profoundly affected by Bloody Sunday; her life was changed by what she witnessed. She has been involved in cross-community and local youth work for many years.

I got really scared coming down William Street — there were Paras positioned on the roofs. When the shooting started, I realised it was real bullets and ran for my life. Alongside me there was a woman in her forties with a scarf. She was praying, 'Jesus, Mary and Joseph, help us,' and the young fellows were cursing and I was sweating — I was terrified. I was trying to run in platform shoes, bell bottoms and long coat.

Hugh Gilmour was right beside me when we were getting over the barricade near the flats. Then the soldiers surged forward again and he was shot. I went to him but when I opened his shirt, I knew it was too late. I had his head on my knees. He was looking for his mother; he told me where he lived and I said, 'Your mother will be down.' He didn't seem to be in pain; he was shocked and shaking. I think he knew himself that he was dying and he started to pray, I said the Act of Contrition. His face relaxed. I couldn't believe it — I'd never seen anybody die before. I didn't want to leave him on his own, I thought if I stayed with him, he would come alive. It was crazy.

I had to take shelter in a corner near a phone box along with ten or eleven others. We were tight to the wall with the Army coming closer, and shooting going on. We could hear somebody crying out that he didn't want to die on his own. And Mr McGuigan says, 'Oh, I can't stand this. If I take a white hanky and go out, they won't shoot me.' We begged him not to go out. He walked out about 6 or 7 feet and as he turned, the bullet hit him; it seemed to be happening in slow motion. His head exploded and his eye came out.

I went hysterical and somebody hit me because he thought I was going to get them all killed. They were so near, we could hear them. A soldier was saying, 'Wait until you have a target! Stop shooting until you have a target!' But all the shooting had finished by that stage. My next recollection after that was in the ambulance.

The next morning, Fr Daly took me down to the Gilmours' house — the grief was terrible. Hugh's mother wanted to know that he was in no pain. She was lovely. They were hugging me and I felt guilty that I was alive. He was the youngest, you see. I couldn't wait to get out of there, I just wanted home, to be safe. I couldn't pass the place for a year-and-a-half.

I went to two wakes: Michael Kelly and John Young. After that I just went home and curled up and wouldn't go out for days. I couldn't go to the chapel or the funerals. I didn't even go to Jackie Duddy's and he was a great friend. For months afterwards, I had panic attacks — I didn't want to tell anybody because I thought I was going cuckoo. I had flashbacks for about three years. I'd start to sweat and my heart would pound and it would all come back. There was nobody you could tell — you couldn't really talk to the families, because you felt that bad about how they were feeling. And I wasn't shot or injured. People expected you to go back to being normal and you were never normal again.

I gave evidence to Widgery and was cross-examined by three people, and I wasn't expecting it because I'd never been in a court before. They were quite adamant, trying to get me to change things, but I knew what I had seen. Widgery said in his Report that I was lying, which devastated me, because I was brought up to believe in truth. I knew it especially hurt my mum. Foremost in my mind was the feeling that I had let down the community.

The Report was a total shock. The whole community didn't know what to do then. They knew that there was this great injustice, but who do you go to? Our whole lives changed after Bloody Sunday. I knew Jim Wray, Willie Nash, John Young, Michael Kelly and Kevin McElhinney — we all used to go to dances. Our age group lost a lot that day. People that had never been involved in political groups joined the IRA because their friends had been killed. It was never the same openness that had been there before.

I had to find resources in myself to come through it, and the way I dealt with it was working with people cross-community. You had to find something good in it, so I worked with International Volunteer Service and I took Catholic and Protestant children to Germany and Holland and London. I got a wild lot from that because I felt there had been too many bridges knocked down and there should be some rebuilt.

I didn't talk to my children about it until the twentieth anniversary, because I think bitterness eats your heart up and if that happened to me, they would have won. I didn't want to put my hurt and sense of injustice into my family.

It took a long time for me to go up to the new Inquiry. I had to get counselling first, before I could even attend it, as I found I wasn't coping very well. I still get flashbacks. It was harrowing, sitting listening to the lawyers talking legal and medical jargon about how people were killed when I actually knew them. I don't want to prejudge Saville and the Inquiry, but it seems that a lot is being put in place to stop it by the MoD. I want the truth told and to tell what I saw.

I would just like this pain to stop.

MAURA YOUNG

Maura Young was 20 years old when her brother, John, was killed in Rossville Street, having been shot in the left eye from a height. John Young was a sociable character — most weekends he was out dancing. He was 17 years old when he died. His brother, Leo, was arrested on Bloody Sunday whilst taking someone to hospital. Upon his release the following morning, ignorant of John's death, he was asked by a policeman how many brothers he had. 'Two,' he replied. Then the policeman said, 'Well you've only one of them now, because we shot the other one yesterday.'

In Rossville Street, standing in the place that John was shot, you try to put yourself beside him to try to stop what happened. It's a strange feeling; it's not a constant thing. But if you're talking about it, something happens: flashbacks of the funeral — very vivid. It takes a few hours to go away. It's very hard, but the more you talk about it, the better; it shaves a wee bit off it, the more you do.

The Saville Inquiry is something that you dreamt of — it was somewhere away.... Now that it's actually happening, I'm still surprised. Some days you'd just be in awe of it. I've been most days in case I missed something — it's not the same reading about it — I'm one of those people who has to see to believe.

He was working in a tailor's — a men's outfitter's. John was very vain about his appearance, loved suits — never owned a pair of jeans in his life. I remember his beautiful black wavy hair. At that time, there was a fad to put Sellotape on your hair to hold it down after you washed it. So I put it on around the back of his neck and at the side of his head. He was sitting waiting for his hair to dry and some girl comes to the door. He went out and he was standing talking to the girl for ages and ages and he forgot about the Sellotape, and when he realised [laughs] ... ach, he called me everything, 'You should have told me....'

I was on the march and when we turned into Rossville Street, I heard rubber bullets and gas canisters being fired. I said to myself, I'm getting off-side, I'd be too afraid in a riot situation. After I got home, my sister Helen came back. 'I was nearly shot,' she said. She was in a terrible state, really upset. She was over at Free Derry Corner when the shooting started — it came from the walls. I went out to the kitchen and made the tea. I'll not make anything for John because he'll probably be late, I thought. Then the news came on. I think the first report was two dead and a few injured. My mother said, 'Dear God, some poor mothers' hearts are going to break.'

Later, I went over to the shop to see where John was. He had girlfriend in England who telephoned him there every Sunday night. He hadn't been in and the woman said, 'You know, there's a lot of people shot down in the town. Maybe you should phone the hospital.' It never dawned on me that this girl probably knew. The word must have filtered up to her in the shop. So I gave her the money for the phone.... She phoned Altnagelvin. She said to me, 'Maura, I think you'll have to go over there.'

I came back to the house and I said to my mother and father, 'I'm going down to Mr Ward to get him to run me over to Altnagelvin.' My father put on his coat and as we were walking down the street I had the strangest feeling, a lonely feeling of something left; it was eerie.

At Altnagelvin Hospital it was a nightmare, it was serious, people everywhere: soldiers, police, blood. Tom O'Gara, the priest, came over and took a list out of his pocket. I remember thinking, Jesus Christ, he has a list of names! 'No, I don't think we have him,' he said. I had a sense of hope which took my breathe away, and I said, 'He's 17, but he looks 22 or 23.' I was waiting for news and ended up sitting on the floor in the corridor. I remember they brought this young fellow out of the treatment room — he was screaming from pain. His arm was hanging out of the bed and there was a hole in his shoulder. The

Gilmours came in looking for their brother and the girl on reception said, 'He's in the morgue.' It was unreal. I think Floyd Gilmour was grappling with a policeman; there was total confusion.

We had him at home in the coffin — he was lovely — aye, he just had a wee grey mark over one of his eyes the size of the top of a cigarette. Thousands of people came to the house; they queued out in the street.

I remember the priest, who came from Creggan Chapel, asking my mother and father if they forgave the soldier. My mother, without batting an eyelid, said, 'I do, that soldier is some mother's son too.' Where do you get courage to say that? She was a very strong, wee woman but it took part of her life away. My father was a very quiet man; he never talked about it. After he died, we found all the newspapers he had collected about it at the back of the drawer in the bedroom.

We had to have tickets to go to our own brother's funeral. We accepted it, sat down and wrote out a list and, believe it or not, we left out my mother's only brother — he couldn't get into the chapel. Fifty tickets per family to go to the funeral. The dignitaries were in the front — they took pride of place; the families were all scattered. It just goes to show you the way we accepted things. Is it any wonder we accepted Widgery? We were totally devastated.

Afterwards, the army raided the house about three times a month until 1973. My father was a chronic asthmatic, and he was in his early sixties when they came one morning at five to arrest him.

I remember my mother crying and she ran up the stairs and there was a wee soldier standing at the top of stairs and she got hold of him. All through that period I never saw my mother show any anger as such. She said, 'You bastard, you murdered my son — now you're going to take my husband!'

My father couldn't get a breath, and this wee soldier knelt down in front of him and tied his shoelaces for him. We drove to the army camp. I had to help him out of the jeep — his legs were awful stiff. I think he aged ten years in that half hour. This soldier came out with pips on his epauletts. He put his hands on his hips and he says, 'What the bloody hell is going on?'

'Only following orders, sir — you told us to arrest whatever men were in the house.'

So he says, 'And you've arrested that man? Let him go.' Then I went over to him and said, 'Do you think he's going to walk back down to Westway from here, at this time of the morning, in the condition he's in? You've brought us up, you will take us back!' Which they did.

We went about everywhere together. John was my best friend; I miss him a wild lot still. At seventeen, he was only starting.... [He] loved his work, loved music, went about with a show band so he could get into the dances. He was very sociable and loved the girls.

BISHOP EDWARD DALY

Edward Daly grew up in Belleek, County Fermanagh. He was ordained in 1957, having studied for the priesthood in Rome. He was appointed curate to Saint Eugene's Cathedral in Derry in 1962. He enjoyed a busy parish life there and got very involved in organising sell-out concerts at the parish hall. An experienced and dedicated priest, he was 34 years old at the time of Bloody Sunday. In his book, Mister, Are You a Priest?, *he recounts his experiences as a curate in Derry before and after Bloody Sunday.*

I was up for early Masses on that Sunday morning, at seven o'clock. From then until six o'clock on Tuesday morning I didn't see my bed.

I went on the march after officiating at a funeral. Rossville Street was in my district. A large number of elderly people lived there. I'd been there for virtually every riot (day and night) that had taken place there since 1969. Those with bronchial problems were very distressed by the CS gas which was often used in vast quantities. They got frightened and on many occasions I found it necessary to evacuate them from the area. But I also identified very much with the objectives of the parade. I vehemently opposed internment. I had visited the internees quite often in the internment camps and I thought it was a profound injustice.

I remember the rioting at the bottom of William Street. It wasn't anything out of the ordinary — par for the course in Derry at that time. As the march came down William Street, I had an uncomfortable feeling. There were Paratroopers on the roofs in sniping positions and that was strange — we'd never seen Paras before in Derry.

The next thing I remember was hearing that someone had been shot. Then I saw armoured cars moving in our direction; they speeded up and panic grew; everybody else was running and I ran with them. In the courtyard of the Rossville Flats I saw Jackie Duddy come running, laughing. I thought he was laughing at me and just at that moment two things happened: he gasped and there was a shot. I thought it was a rubber bullet. People were trying to [get] through the doorway of the flats; panic was developing. There were other shots and I dived behind a low wall about 18 inches high, where I took cover with a large number of people. All hell was let loose.

The firing was all coming from the Paras and nowhere else. I was anxious about Jackie and I peeked out a couple of times. He was lying there still; I knew then it wasn't a rubber bullet. In situations like that, a short period of time seems like an eternity. Eventually, there was a lull in the firing. I was terrified as I got out beside him. There was a lot of blood; I opened his shirt and tried to staunch the bleeding with a handkerchief. Then a member of the Knights of Malta, Charlie Glenn, arrived out beside me and said, 'He's very badly injured,' so I decided to administer the last rites. I got out my oils and anointed him. We both had to lie down because the gunfire was quite heavy. Most of the time we were on our tummies. Now I wonder would I have gone out under gunfire if had time to think about it; [laughs] I think you have an innate duty to do those things. But when we were out there in that courtyard, really we were in deep trouble.

A guy came out to our right and he started dancing hysterically up and down, waving his arms and shouting at the soldiers. I saw a soldier lift his rifle and fire. [The guy] was injured — it was Michael Bridge. Then a man appeared briefly with a gun beside the gable wall at the end of Chamberlain Street and fired. He was the only civilian I saw with a gun that day. Gradually, we were joined by Willy Barber and then Liam Bradley. We decided we'd have to get [Jackie] to hospital as quickly as possible. They suggested that I go in front with a white handkerchief. I'd never seen anybody waving one before, except to surrender in films, but they suggested that it might afford some protection. So,

we made a dash for the mouth of Chamberlain Street. We walked out of the frying pan into the fire. We didn't realise there were soldiers firing towards us from Chamberlain Street. But we had to get Jackie out. We weren't going to drop him there — that would have been criminal. It was just as we were turning up Harvey Street that Cyril Cave, the BBC cameraman, filmed us. We laid Jackie on the ground outside McHugh's shop.

Mrs McHugh phoned for an ambulance but [Jackie] was dead. So he died somewhere on that journey. She made us tea; I took one sip and then people came running, 'Come quick, come quick.' The sight I saw, I couldn't believe. There were dead and injured all over the place. So I anointed and administered last rites to everyone. I could see three dead bodies: one of them was Barney McGuigan lying in a pool of blood. Young Nash's father was shot too. I thought that what I'd seen was shocking and horrendous. I had no idea that this had been repeated in Rossville Street and in Glenfada Park at the same time, and that, in fact, they were still shooting people. I have no idea how many I anointed that day. Fathers Tony Mulvey and Tom O'Gara were attending to people also. I discovered subsequently that other priests were there too.

The enormity of what had happened didn't sink in until about half-past four and [at] the first interview I gave; I'm almost certain it was John Berman from the BBC who interviewed me on the spot. He was shattered too by what he'd seen. Barney McGuigan's body had just been taken away in an ambulance.

Our parochial house was packed with people that night. About a hundred people were arrested; the authorities wouldn't release their names. Everybody who hadn't accounted for a member of the family immediately thought the worst. There was confusion — for example, young McDaid's body was identified as somebody else. I remember Mrs McDaid coming along and being assured that he must have been arrested. She hadn't left our house 20 minutes when we heard that her son was dead. That night is like a blur. We were visiting houses all night, trying to comfort people. A huge silence came down over the city. Monday was spent with grieving relatives; the post-mortems were taking place; we were visiting the injured in hospital. Gradually some of the bodies were released and brought home. Tuesday was spent visiting wakes all over the town. The city came to a standstill commercially and industrially. On Wednesday there were the funerals. There was one Requiem Mass for all the dead in St Mary's Church in Creggan, as it was the biggest available church and most of the victims were from that parish. Thirteen different funerals would have been an intolerable emotional burden for everybody.

As a result of a request from the Irish Government, I was on a plane to America on the Thursday. I gave a big press conference the following morning in New York. I had met Jack Lynch in Dublin on the Monday night when I gave a television interview on a programme called *Seven Days*. He was in the studios to give a speech to the nation. He said, 'I'm very concerned that the British are putting across a completely distorted version in the United States.' They had issued a statement saying a number of people who had died were on the wanted list.

I had never been to America before. I did nearly all the morning shows like *Good Morning America* and all the networks: CBS, NBC and ABC. The Americans had bought the British version of the story, hook, line and sinker — that was an eye-opener. They were getting the London version of almost everything because there wasn't a single US wire service source on the island of Ireland — their offices were in London.

In New York, I was staying in the Roosevelt Hotel where several scenes in *The French Connection* were filmed, and that fascinated me because I'm a film buff. Then I flew to Los Angeles where I stopped in the Beverly Wilshire Hotel. I was goggle-eyed. I think I was running on adrenalin because there was always another interview to do. I came back to Derry completely exhausted. I remember I spent a couple of days in bed recovering. There was the emotional trauma as well. I suppose, in modern parlance, I never had time to grieve, but I did have the opportunity to talk endlessly about it. That's one of the best therapies, talking it out of your system.

The next thing was the dilemma of whether or not to appear at Widgery. A lot of people said that Widgery was going to be a whitewash. I thought that too. The relatives were divided on the issue. After being traumatised by the experience of Bloody Sunday, it was very hard to make any kind of objective decision. But the American experience had been educational because I saw there the power of the media. Myself and the other priests had long debates. Tony Mulvey and I felt that if we did not appear before Widgery ... our colleagues in England would say, 'There they were speaking on television, but they're not prepared to swear it on oath.' We felt we should go before Widgery and bear witness. I've no regrets about it. Had we not spoken, there

would have been no counsel to cross-examine the Paras and to show them up for liars. They totally contradicted their own evidence, yet Widgery's report did not reflect this.

The Cathedral was a very busy place and there were more shootings that year. It was terrible. There wasn't time to hold your breath. I think we tried to cope by the ministry of our work, with prayer and the help of colleagues, which was a great support. But I did crack up eventually in 1973. I got hepatitis and was quite ill. The doctor recommended me to get out of Derry for a while. So I went to work at RTÉ, in Dublin. I felt like a fish out of water because I missed the warmth of the North. I was getting accustomed to Dublin when I was appointed as Bishop of Derry, so I suddenly found myself back here seven or eight months later. The break was helpful.

The result of the Saville Inquiry is too early to call. The evidence from the soldiers and the people who had control of them ... is possibly the most interesting aspect. I think it will be very difficult to get at the truth, and that worries me. I have attended the Inquiry and was quite concerned at the hostile questioning by Army counsel of some of the civilian witnesses, particularly when they had nobody there to stand up for them. I insisted that I had counsel at the Tribunal when I came to give evidence; to my amazement, very few people have done that. I felt reassured by his presence, though he never intervened. While I have my own needs to tell the story, one has to speak for a lot of people; I feel that burden very much — for Jackie Duddy particularly — but also for my colleagues, Tony Mulvey and Tom O'Gara. Those of us who were witnesses have a duty to ensure that the good names of the victims be reinstated.

ST. MARY'S CHURCH

FUNERAL

Wednesday, 2nd February, 1972

EACH OF THE FAMILIES OF THE DEAD RECEIVED FIFTY OF THESE FUNERAL
TICKETS FOR THE REQUIEM MASS THAT WAS HELD FOR THOSE WHO DIED
ON BLOODY SUNDAY.

EPILOGUE

I feel it is vital to take account of the views of those most affected by events of this nature, as well as other, wider perspectives; history is full of silent victims. Their humanity is denied. Often they are not regarded as sentient beings. They have been pulled into the current of history and forced to respond to an unwanted turn of events with what resources they have to hand. Many of those in this book spoke of anger and forgiveness — two responses, which, importantly, are not mutually exclusive. It was both love and rage that impelled some of them to risk the rejection of an indifferent world and campaign to clear the names of their loved ones. The Saville Inquiry has been one more stage in this process.

What I have found most striking is how the sense of family and belonging played a big rôle in reining in the madness of grief. People talked of seeing someone 'coming around'; by that they meant becoming more accepting of their bereavement. They also meant a kind of coming back to one's senses. Some dealt with their loss by sharing the pain and trying to live in the everyday present. Faith and spirituality could often be great ballast when anguish drove a person beyond what they could bear.

According to Widgery, there were twenty-seven official victims of Bloody Sunday; but there is also Daniel Gillespie, who was shot but didn't go to hospital. So the true total is twenty-eight. It also must be remembered that there were thousands at the actual event, and many still carry the memories of a day on which it became a capital offence to go on a civil rights demonstration.

GLOSSARY

Altnagelvin Hospital	City hospital located on the east bank of the River Foyle.
B Specials	Armed auxiliary police force (almost entirely Protestant) which was abolished in 1969 and replaced by the Ulster Defence Regiment.
Battle of the Bogside	Three days of rioting and major confrontation between residents of the Bogside, on the one hand, and the RUC and loyalist mobs, on the other, at the time of the annual Protestant Apprentice Boys March on 12 August 1969.
Bloody Sunday Justice Campaign	An action group formed in April 1992 by relatives of the victims of Bloody Sunday in order to establish the truth of what happened and ensure justice for the dead and injured.
Bogside	(Also known as 'The Bog') A predominantly Catholic quarter located on the west side of Derry below the city walls and built on an area of peat bog.
Bogside Community Association	A body elected by 12,000 local people to represent community interests of the Bogside, Creggan and Brandywell areas after the events of Bloody Sunday and Operation Motorman.
Brandywell	A predominantly Catholic area adjacent to the Bogside.
Brits	Colloquial term for the British Army and/or establishment.
Craic	Colloquial term for 'having a good time'.
Creggan	A predominantly Catholic housing estate on a hillside above the Bogside.
Derry Housing Action Committee	A group of housing rights activists, formed in the Bogside in early 1968, and which employed tactics of direct action to protest against discriminatory housing policies.
Derry Walls	The city walls built by English military forces between 1614 and 1618 to protect the city from invasion. They stand in their entirety today, and enclose what is still the city centre.
Dum-dum Bullet	A colloquial term for ammunition that has been illegally tampered with. The bullet cases are filed at the head to maximise injury to the victim.

Ford, Major General	British Army Commander, Land Forces, at the time of Bloody Sunday.
Fort George	British Army base located in Strand Road on the northern outskirts of the city.
Free Derry	First 'no-go area' in Northern Ireland, established initially in January 1969, and more permanently in August of that year, after the Battle of the Bogside.
Free Derry Corner	Location at the gable-end of a terraced house in the Bogside, painted with the slogan 'You Are Now Entering Free Derry', and regularly used for open-air meetings.
Glenfada Park	A small estate of low-rise flats situated across the street from the Rossville Flats.
High Flats	An alternative name for the Rossville Flats.
Internment	Imprisonment without trial. It was introduced in Northern Ireland on 9 August 1971, and the march on Bloody Sunday was in protest against it.
Knights of Malta	Voluntary corps of first-aid workers.
Lynch, Jack	Taoiseach (Prime Minister) of the Republic of Ireland at the time of Bloody Sunday.
MoD	The British Ministry of Defence.
Motorman	Short for Operation Motorman, the biggest British military operation since Suez. On 31 August 1972, 12,000 troops supported, by tanks and bulldozers, smashed their way into the no-go areas of Derry. Two civilians were shot dead in the process.
No-Go Areas	Areas in Northern Ireland that were barricaded and patrolled by local residents, and which were effectively out of bounds to the British Army and the RUC.
NICRA	Northern Ireland Civil Rights Association, established in 1967.
Old IRA	The original Irish Republican Army, established to fight against British rule in Ireland during the War of Independence (1919–1921).
Paras	Short for Parachute Regiment, a crack regiment of the British Army reputed to be its toughest.
Provisional IRA	('Provos') Militant wing of the IRA which broke away from the original organisation in 1969 as a result of disagreement over how to act in response to the Troubles.
Rossville Flats	Three blocks of high-rise flats, located between Rossville Street and Fahan Street at the time of Bloody Sunday, and subsequently demolished.
Royal Anglian Regiment	A British Army regiment stationed in Derry at the time of Bloody Sunday, some of whom were positioned on the City Walls during the march.

RUC	Royal Ulster Constabulary — predominantly Protestant, armed police force of Northern Ireland. The year 2001 saw the introduction of the Police Service of Northern Ireland.
Saracen	An armed troop-carrier used by the British Army and sometimes referred to as a 'pig'.
Troubles, The	Popular term used to refer to the period of Irish history commencing in 1968 with the campaign for civil rights in Northern Ireland, and ending with the Provisional IRA's declaration of a cease-fire in 1994.
Tuzo, Lieutenant General	The British Army General Officer Commanding Northern Ireland at the time of Bloody Sunday.
Widgery (Tribunal)	British Government Inquiry into the events of Bloody Sunday chaired by Lord Widgery whose report was published on 18 April 1971. It was widely regarded as a 'whitewash', especially by the Catholic community.
Wilford, Lieutenant Colonel Derek	The officer in charge of the Parachute Regiment on Bloody Sunday. He was later awarded an OBE for his activities in Derry that day.

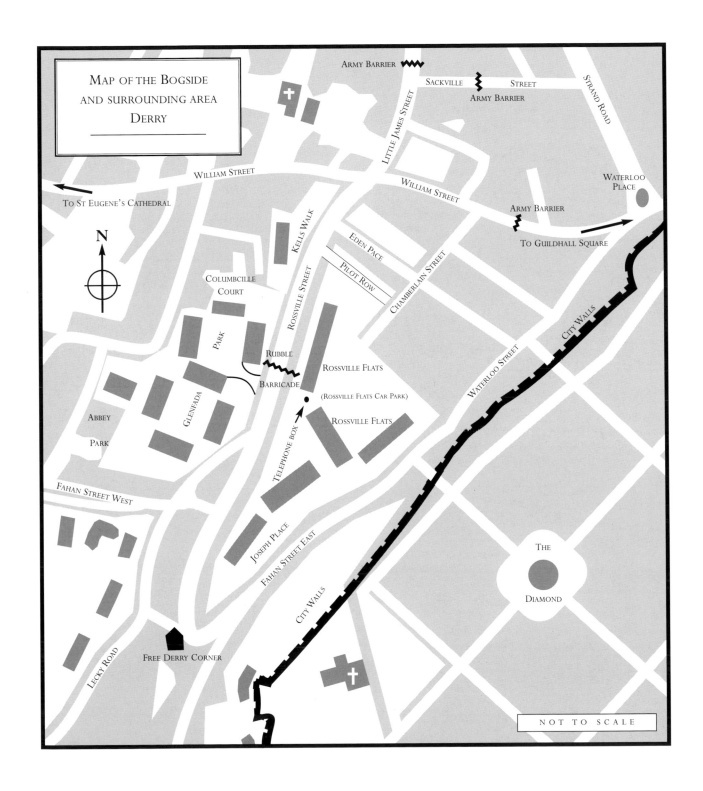

MAP OF THE BOGSIDE
AND SURROUNDING AREA
DERRY

ARMY BARRIER

SACKVILLE   STREET
ARMY BARRIER

STRAND ROAD

LITTLE JAMES STREET

WILLIAM STREET

WILLIAM STREET

WATERLOO
PLACE

TO ST EUGENE'S CATHEDRAL

ARMY BARRIER

TO GUILDHALL SQUARE

N

KELLS WALK

EDEN PACE

PILOT ROW

CHAMBERLAIN STREET

COLUMBCILLE
COURT

ROSSVILLE STREET

CITY WALLS

WATERLOO STREET

PARK

RUBBLE

BARRICADE

ROSSVILLE FLATS

(ROSSVILLE FLATS CAR PARK)

ROSSVILLE FLATS

GLENFADA

ABBEY

PARK

TELEPHONE BOX

FAHAN STREET WEST

THE

JOSEPH PLACE

FAHAN STREET EAST

DIAMOND

CITY WALLS

LECKY ROAD

FREE DERRY CORNER

NOT TO SCALE

INDEX